DAMNING ASSUMPTIONS

What Advocates of Endless Torment Take for Granted

Max H. Sotak

New Reformation Books

DAMNING ASSUMPTIONS:
What Advocates of Endless Torment Take For Granted
Max H. Sotak

ISBN: 978-0-9896808-0-6

© 2013 Max H. Sotak. All rights reserved worldwide.

Published by: New Reformation Books

No part of this publication may be reproduced, stored in a retrieval system, or transmitted in any form or by any means—for example, electronics, photocopy, recording—without the prior written permission of the publisher. The only exception is brief quotations in printed reviews.

Scripture taken from the HOLY BIBLE, NEW INTERNATIONAL VERSION.
Copyright © 1973, 1978, 1984 International Bible Society.
Used by permission of Zondervan Bible Publishers.

CONTENTS

Preface v

Introduction: Is Endless Torment The Obvious
    Biblical View? 1

Chapter 1: Man's Immortality: A Gift of
    Creation or Salvation? 17

Chapter 2: Favorite Arguments for
    Endless Torment 33

Chapter 3: Eternal Things That Don't
    Last Forever 55

Conclusion: Is Conditional Immortality a Heresy? ... 77

Bibliography 93

PREFACE

Belief in the endless torment of those without Christ is viewed by many Christians as a hallmark of orthodoxy. For centuries, this view has been the majority position of those who take the Bible and sin seriously. Majority views, however, are not always true. At the time of the Reformation, justification by faith plus meritorious works was the majority view. We are grateful today that the Reformers understood that majorities often make mistakes. Against great opposition, they forged a better proclamation of the gospel in the light of biblical truth.

The problem with majorities is that they sometimes behave like monopolies, underestimating the competition because of their secure position in the marketplace. The argument of this book is that advocates of endless torment have made this mistake. Instead of considering seriously the problems raised by their opponents, they have often relied on the recycled arguments of the past without subjecting them to legitimate criticism.

What view do I offer in place of endless torment? Conditional immortality is an important and persuasive minority position on the subject of eternal judgment. As the label indicates, immortality is to be found only in Christ (2 Tim. 1:10). Therefore, those who reject Christ do not continue to live forever in a state of endless suffering because of the indestructibility of their souls. As Jesus said, God is able to destroy both body and soul in hell (Matt. 10:28), and so the lost will face their final destruction after a just period of penal suffering in hell. For those who think that the majority position is obvious, I offer the challenge that it is certainly not as obvious as you may have been led to think. Once the damning assumptions behind the doctrine of endless torment are exposed, you may find yourself more sympathetic to conditional immortality and to the Evangelicals who have embraced it as the truth of God's Word.

Introduction

IS ENDLESS TORMENT THE OBVIOUS BIBLICAL VIEW?

A Troubling Doctrine

The doctrine of endless torment in the lake of fire is the most disturbing of all religious beliefs; it is also considered by many to be the easiest doctrine to prove from the Bible. Among Christian denominations that consider the Bible the inspired Word of God, most believe that faithfulness to the Bible requires submission to the traditional belief that the damned will suffer the torments of hell forever. Because of an infinite load of guilt for their sins, they can never be purged of their guilt or destroyed by the fire. While traditionalists[1] do not generally find it easy

---

[1] For the sake of simplicity, advocates of the doctrine of endless conscious torment will be referred to as traditionalists, and the position itself will be referred to as the traditional view. I realize that the word *traditionalist* can carry a negative connotation, referring to someone who puts tradition above the teaching of the Bible. This is rarely, however, the intent of those who

to speak freely and openly about this ominous doctrine, some are very candid about the implications of their belief:

> If the Holy Spirit does not act to bring revival in our generation, the vast majority of these people [the five to six billion people alive in the world today] will be resurrected with perfect bodies to experience an eternity of screaming agony in the lake of fire, tortured without mercy by the God of the Bible forever (Rev. 20:14-15).[2]

Traditionalists seldom use this kind of language today because it is offensive to those they are trying to win to the Christian faith. A God who will torture the lost without mercy forever is not very attractive to people living after "the century of megadeath," in which an estimated 87,000,000 people have been killed by war and countless others have been wounded, tortured, and maimed.[3] There is, however, another reason for the curious neglect of the traditional view of hell—those who hold the doctrine are personally troubled by it:

> I believe, in other words, in the endless conscious pain caused by the absence of everything good, but this

---

      advocate the doctrine of endless torment. Most believe it because they are convinced the Bible teaches it. The fact that it is also the majority view of historic Christianity is considered a plus for the position, but it is certainly not the main reason believers embrace it.

[2]   Gary North, letter to ICE subscribers, Feb. 1996. This author also refers to Jesus Christ as "the cosmic torturer and terrorist." In doing so, he believes he is being consistent with what the Bible actually teaches about final punishment.

[3]   Zbigniew Brzezinski, *Out of Control: Global Turmoil on the Eve of the Twenty-First Century* (New York: Collier Books, 1993) 10.

> thought is so unbearable that I can only take consolation in God's goodness and in the hope of conversion.[4]

This is a strange confession and illustrates a tension present in many Christian minds. On the one hand, the author is convinced that God is good, and yet he finds the justice of God, as he understands it, unbearable. Logically, if God is good so is his justice, in which case the endless pain of the damned is also good. The logical response would be to rejoice in the justice of God, not to find it unbearable. After all, if the eternal torment of the lost will not disturb our heavenly bliss, then why should it disturb us now?

Roger Nicole, a well-known defender of the traditional view, senses the inconsistency between our present and future attitudes toward hell and attempts to justify them:

> But doesn't the eternal existence of a dark spot in the universe spoil the bliss of the redeemed in heaven and of the triune God himself? How can we be happy in heaven knowing that many are suffering in hell? This objection does not sufficiently consider the heinousness of sin and the importance of God's honor whose majesty has been violated by our disobedience. *From the vantage point of heaven and of divine holiness, the sheer ugliness of sin will be fully apparent and will undoubtedly erase remnants of*

---

[4] Scott McKnight, "Eternal Consequences or Eternal Consciousness?", *Through No Fault of their Own*, ed. William V. Crockett and James G. Sigountos (Grand Rapids: Baker Book House, 1991) 148.

natural affection that were appropriate on the earth scene (emphasis mine).[5]

Nicole believes that the reason we have a natural affection for the lost in this life is that we do not sense the full seriousness of sin as an offense to God. This natural affection is somehow appropriate here on earth, despite the fact that it is based on an inadequate view of sin. Even more striking is the fact that heaven will supposedly erase our natural affection for the lost! The point of this is shocking: The motivation to evangelize is based on a compassion for the lost that the fully sanctified saint in heaven does not have and should not have, according to Nicole. So the closer to perfection we get the less natural affection for the lost we have. Does this mean that God is making use of our lack of sanctification to get the job of missions done?

These points alone should be enough to cause Christians to question whether or not they have correctly understood the biblical teaching on final judgment. Unfortunately, most traditionalists are led to believe that questioning the doctrine of endless torment is tantamount to making common cause with cults and humanists. There are, however, many well-known Christian scholars of evangelical persuasion who are questioning the traditional view on biblical as well as moral grounds. Could it be that the Bible really does not teach that the lost will suffer forever? Could

---

[5] Roger Nicole, "Universalism: Will Everyone Be Saved?" *Christianity Today* 20 Mar. 1987: 38.

it be that the Bible is saying instead that those outside the Christian fold will be punished to the extent that their sins deserve and then terminated forever? Could it be that immortality is conditioned upon faith in Christ and not our creation as immortal beings?[6] While most Christians would love to say yes to each of these questions, they have been led by traditional arguments to believe that the Bible simply will not allow it. The truth is that the Bible not only allows us to believe in the final extinction of the lost, but it demands it if we are to do justice to the coherence of the Christian Scriptures.

A Troubled Doctrine

Endless torment is not being questioned today just because of an aversion to the Bible's teachings.[7] There are principles of justice within the Bible itself that seem to contradict the idea that finite sins committed in this life

---

[6] "By way of *definition*: belief in conditional immortality is the belief that God created Man only potentially immortal. Immortality is a state gained by grace through faith when the believer receives eternal life and becomes a partaker of the divine nature, immortality being inherent in God alone." John Wenham, "The Case for Conditional Immortality", *Universalism and the Doctrine of Hell*, ed. Nigel M. Cameron (Grand Rapids: Baker Book House, 1992) 161-162.

[7] It is important to consider why a person questions the doctrine of eternal torment. Some people really do not care what the Bible teaches; they will reject anything in the Bible they find objectionable. Others are questioning traditional interpretations of the Bible because they believe them to be flawed, not because they think the Bible is flawed. Evangelical conditionalists are certainly in this second camp. Few traditionalists have bothered to take note of this critical distinction, although a few have. cf. Robert L. Reymond, "Dr. John Stott on Hell", *Presbyterion: Covenant Seminary Review* 16 (1990): 42.

deserve infinite punishing.[8] Common sense also brings us into conflict with the traditional view. If every sin creates an infinite debt of guilt before God, then how can there be degrees of punishment at all, since each sin deserves an infinite punishment? And what of practical matters of guilt and punishment that must be dealt with in social contexts? The common belief that the punishment must fit the crime is truly biblical, but how can we assess appropriate punishments if every sin involves infinite guilt? The truth is that human justice never operates on the principle of infinite guilt; it always operates on the principle of finite guilt. Every crime has a punishment that is appropriate to it in intensity and duration. This idea, by the way, comes right out of the Law of Moses (Ex. 21:23-25). Even Christians, then, are logically led to question the traditional view's assumption of infinite guilt just by reading their own Bible.

Unfortunately, the defenders of endless torment have argued that only liberals or sentimentalists would ever question their view.[9] Those who argue for the final

---

[8] This is probably the key assumption of the traditional position. Interestingly, the Bible never makes the point—implicitly or explicitly—that finite sins against an infinite God deserve an infinite punishment. The truth is that this idea is really an implication of the traditional position, not an argument for it. Traditionalists unintentionally mislead their listeners by presenting this assumption as an argument when it is a mere assumption. In doing so, they commit the fallacy of begging the question, or circular reasoning.

[9] The charge of a sentimental view of God's love is a gross distortion of the conditionalist position. The unfairness and inaccuracy of this charge is shockingly evident in these words of Millard Erickson, a theologian who generally excels all others in fairness and honesty: "Pinnock, Stott, and others depict a sentimentalized version [of God's love], in which God would

extinction of the lost are dismissed out of hand since, they say, the traditional view is so obvious.[10] Why have so many believed them? The answer is simple: Most traditionalists have never read or heard a serious biblical defense of conditional immortality by an evangelical who believes it. Instead, the arguments of conditionalists are presented by traditionalists in a popular and abbreviated form so they can be disposed of without much difficulty. Most evangelicals are exposed to conditional immortality by reading books about cults. This leads them to conclude that only a cultist would advocate conditional immortality since there are some cults that do.[11]

Readers of the traditionalist literature are easily left with the impression that no one has presented a good case against their position because they never see a major book by a conditionalist. Many probably believe that traditional scholars have established their position so solidly that no one dares to reply. But such is not the case. The truth is that evangelical conditionalists cannot get their books published

> not do anything that would cause anyone pain, displeasure, or discomfort. Thus, endless suffering would be incompatible with divine love." Millard J. Erickson, *How Shall They Be Saved* (Grand Rapids: Baker Book House, 1996) 227. According to conditionalists, God is doing and will do a great deal to cause pain, displeasure, and discomfort for the lost. Conditionalists affirm the justice of God in creating hell as a place of "weeping and gnashing of teeth." The problem is not pain but endless pain. To say that conditionalists believe that "God would not do anything to cause pain" is a blatant misrepresentation. This kind of distortion is unworthy of a fine evangelical scholar like Erickson.

[10] cf. Robert Morey, *Death and the Afterlife* (Minneapolis: Bethany House Publishers, 1984) 15-16.

[11] However, reading about cults has not led evangelicals to conclude that only a cultist would advocate premillennialism because many modern cults are premillennial.

because evangelical publishers have been closed minded on the subject. John Wenham, a well-known British evangelical discusses his experience with this problem:

> Matters reached a crisis point in 1973, when I presented Inter-Varsity Press with the MS of *The Goodness of God*. IVP had already published my *Christ and the Bible*, which I had let them have on condition that they would publish its sequel, concerning the moral difficulties of the Bible. I thought hell was too big a subject to treat in this book and decided simply to content myself with presenting the biblical images without comment. IVP sent the MS to a discerning reader who then asked for help on this topic. So I wrote half-a-dozen pages advocating conditional immortality. At this IVP were up in arms and a long correspondence ensued which ended with a conference with some of their senior people. I was astonished at how little they had thought about the subject. But at least we were agreed that the biblical research which we were promoting should be more concerned about fundamental doctrines than archaeological minutiae and they allowed me to try to state both doctrines as fairly as I could. This was a great step forward for neither Atkinson nor Guillebaud had been able to find a publisher. So I have been waiting since 1973 for a reply to the massive work of Froom (2,476 pages), to Atkinson's closely argued 112 pages, to Guillebaud's 67 and (more important) to the one additional book which has appeared on the conditionalist side: Edward Fudge's *The Fire That Consumes*.[12]

---

[12] Wenham 163-164.

Wenham goes on to mention four books that were released between 1986 and 1990 that attempted to answer the arguments of conditionalists. Wenham's response to these replies is that none of them actually address the arguments used by conditionalists.[13] Lest it be thought that Wenham is just crying "sour grapes," it should be pointed out that conditionalists are not the only ones who feel that traditionalists and their publishers are not giving the position a fair hearing. Consider the words of Kendall Harmon, a defender of the traditional position:

> John Wenham's plea stems from an important motivation, however, which is that the arguments for conditionalism have not been heard by many traditionalists. In my combining of the literature of the last hundred years I would say that very often this has been the case, particularly because conditionalists have not been able to find mainstream publishers for their work.[14]

A crucial turning point came in 1988 with the publication of the book, *Evangelical Essentials: A Liberal-Evangelical Dialogue*, co-authored by David Edwards and John Stott.[15] In that book, Stott presents the major arguments for conditional immortality and concludes his

---

[13] Wenham 165.

[14] Kendall S. Harmon, "The Case Against Conditionalism: A Response to Edward William Fudge", *Universalism and the Doctrine of Hell*, ed. Nigel M. Cameron (Grand Rapids: Baker Book House, 1992) 201n.

[15] David L. Edwards and John R Stott, *Evangelical Essentials: A Liberal-Evangelical Dialogue* (Downers Grove: InterVarsity Press, 1988).

discussion with the following advice:

> I do not dogmatise about the position to which I have come. I hold it tentatively. But I do plead for frank dialogue among Evangelicals on the basis of Scripture. I also believe that the ultimate annihilation of the wicked should at least be accepted as a legitimate, biblically founded alternative to their eternal conscious torment.[16]

This advice, coming from one of evangelicalism's most highly respected scholars, has probably done more than anything else to break down the traditional bias against conditional immortality and to cause evangelicals to consider the biblical arguments in its favor. Many of those who heed this good advice will realize that the doctrine of endless torment is not the solid rock they thought it was. Upon closer examination, it will become clear that the traditional view really cannot do justice to much of what the Bible teaches about final punishment.

The Trouble With Doctrine

Many Christians approach the Bible in a simplistic way and assume that determining what the Bible teaches on any subject is just a matter of adding up a series of proof texts. The problem is that many Christian doctrines are not so simple and uncomplicated. The reason that some issues are difficult to discern in the Bible is that the biblical writers often express themselves in ways quite different from our

---
[16] Edwards and Stott 320.

own ways of speaking. For example, biblical writers often use hyperbole (pronounced *hi-per-bo-lee*) in much more striking ways than we do. Hyperbole is intentional overstatement for the sake of emotional effect. Jesus said, "If anyone comes to me and does not hate his father and mother, his wife and children, his brothers and sisters— yes, even his own life—he cannot be my disciple (Lk. 14:26). Jesus did not literally mean that we should hate our parents, for if he did, he would have been contradicting the fifth commandment, which commands that parents be honored. He also did not mean to say that we should literally hate our own lives, since that would contradict the second great commandment, which commands that we love our neighbor as ourselves. This command assumes a certain legitimate self-love that defines our duty to our neighbor. Using hyperbole, Jesus was saying that we cannot put any earthly relationship above our allegiance to him.

Biblical language can also be understood in more than one sense. For example, Matthew 3:12 refers to an "unquenchable fire." Is an unquenchable fire a fire that never stops or a fire that cannot be stopped before it consumes its fuel? Both senses are compatible with the phrase, but how do we determine which is intended by the biblical author? Generally issues of context and the relationship of other passages on the subject come into play here to enable us to discern the intent of the Bible as a whole. But this is not a simple matter, especially when talking about the subject of final judgment.

The controversy between traditionalists and conditionalists on the subject of hell is really a controversy about how the Bible's judgment language should be harmonized.[17] There are passages in the Bible that can be understood as traditionalists have understood them. The problem is that there are many other passages that simply do not fit the assumption that the lost will suffer endlessly in a fire that never destroys them. Matthew 3:12 is a good example to illustrate the disagreement between traditionalists and conditionalists: "His winnowing fork is in his hand, and he will clear his threshing floor, gathering his wheat into the barn and burning up the chaff with unquenchable fire." John the Baptist is speaking here of the Messiah's salvation and judgment. John says that the chaff, referring to the wicked, will be burned up. To conditionalists, this clearly suggests the termination of the wicked, since fire disintegrates what it burns. Taking the words at face value, we would conclude that final judgment will result in

---

[17] I held the traditional position for seventeen years before undertaking a study of conditionalist literature. Prior to that time, all my exposure to conditionalists was second hand. To my surprise, I found that the traditionalists that I had read extensively did not present the case for conditional immortality as thoroughly or as clearly as the conditionalists themselves. Even before I was fully satisfied that the traditional view is unbiblical, it became clear to me that the controversy revolves around hermeneutics and the harmony of the Bible. Traditionalists I had read portrayed conditionalists as liberals who simply refused to accept the Bible's clear teachings. They did not deal with the conditionalists' exegesis of key passages, nor did they mention the conditionalists' criticisms of their own exegesis. One can come away with the impression that traditionalists do not think they need to address their opponents' arguments. This, in my opinion, is the reason that conditionalist arguments keep coming back to pester the traditionalists—traditionalists simply have never refuted the arguments of conditionalists, but they continue to insist that they have!

ultimate annihilation. Traditionalists, however, focus on the words "unquenchable fire." They assume that an unquenchable fire is a fire that never stops, so the chaff must continue to exist in order to be burned forever, despite the fact that the image used here would seem to suggest consumption (asbestos chaff?). Conditionalists respond by saying that an unquenchable fire is simply a fire that cannot be stopped before it accomplishes its purpose, so there need be no conflict between the image of chaff being consumed and the unstoppable fire that consumes it. Traditionalists, on the other hand, do not do justice to both images and thereby introduce a tension within the judgment language. This is only one example; many others will be cited later as further evidence of this point.

In fairness to traditionalists, it must be acknowledged that this one example does not do justice to the complexity of their argument. There are passages that seem to teach endless conscious torment at first glance. Each of these must be dealt with in order to show why they really do not support the traditional position. The illustration above, however, does get at the heart of the difference between the two positions. The controversy about hell is about how we harmonize the Bible.[18] It is not really about who is twisting

---

[18] While traditionalists are often willing to acknowledge that controversial issues reflect differences in hermeneutical paradigms, they avoid doing so when it comes to the subject of hell. Perhaps this is due to the fact that their position is usually defended in a simple proof-text fashion with little discussion of hermeneutical presuppositions. Also, endless torment has been the majority position, so most are reluctant to tear up the floor to see if the foundation is really intact. In reading traditional literature, it becomes obvious that advocates of endless torment have been handing their arguments down to

the Bible and who is not; it is about who is doing the best job interpreting the language the Bible uses to describe final judgment. It is a controversy about assumptions and whether the Bible supports the assumptions that interpreters bring to it. The traditional position is certainly top-heavy when it comes to assumptions about judgment that are brought to the Bible. Each one will be examined in light of the Bible to see if it is shared by the biblical writers. In many cases, it will become clear that the key assumptions traditionalists make are nowhere to be found in the Christian scriptures.

In attacking the doctrine of endless torment, conditionalists hope to save the doctrine of hell from becoming a theological museum piece. The traditional view is laden with a number of false assumptions that harm the testimony of the Christian Church. The doctrine of universalism (the belief that everyone will eventually be saved) is really a reaction to the extremity of the traditional view. As long as orthodoxy is defined in terms of endless torment, universalism will continue to silence the biblical threats of final punishment for sin. Hyperorthodoxy always provokes an equally extreme and unbiblical reaction. Conditionalists provide a balanced position that satisfies both the justice of God and the mercy of God. Without such a balanced position, traditionalists will continue to

---

each other for generations with little or no self-criticism. They will not find it easy or comfortable, therefore, to begin questioning a long standing tradition. Conservatism, by its very nature, tends to fear and oppose progress. A reasonable caution is good, but taken too far it can also lead to obscurantism, which opposes self-examination and positive biblical reforms.

offend God by their misrepresentation of his justice, and universalists will continue to offend God by their misrepresentation of his mercy. John Wenham summarizes in strong language the urgency of the case for conditional immortality:

> I believe that endless torment is a hideous and unscriptural doctrine which has been a terrible burden on the mind of the church for many centuries and a terrible blot on her presentation of the gospel. I should indeed be happy if, before I die, I could help in sweeping it away.[19]

The arguments that follow are offered in the belief that the sentiments of Dr. Wenham are justified.

---

[19] Wenham 190.

Chapter 1
MAN'S IMMORTALITY: A GIFT OF CREATION OR SALVATION?

At the heart of human destiny is a question every Christian asks: Is immortality a natural endowment of the soul? Most agree that the body is naturally mortal, but through Christ and the resurrection it can become immortal. But is the soul naturally immortal? Will it survive to all eternity, despite the ravages of sin, the fires of hell, or the wrath of God to destroy it? All orthodox Christians believe that the soul survives the body. This is really not what is at issue. What is at issue is whether or not the wicked suffer forever, body and soul, in the lake of fire.

Throughout Christian history, the answer to this question has often been determined by the belief that humans were created with an immortal soul. Because each person was created with an immortal soul, even the fires of hell will not destroy it. In short, the nature of the soul requires an eternal conscious torment. In fairness to traditionalists, it must be acknowledged that not all have argued in this way. Many modern advocates of endless torment realize that the traditional arguments for an immortal soul reflect pagan thought rather than biblical thought, so they build their argument differently.[20] Robert Peterson, for example, bases his belief in an immortal soul on his belief in endless torment:

> Finally, and most importantly, I do not believe in the traditional view of hell because I accept the immortality of human beings, but the other way around. I believe in the immortality of human beings because the Bible clearly teaches everlasting damnation for the wicked and everlasting life for the righteous.[21]

This is certainly a better approach than some traditionalists use, but it also has some significant problems because it continues to affirm the soul's immortality. According to the biblical usage of the word *immortal*, referring to a soul in hell as immortal is simply a misnomer. Because of the different ways traditionalists use the idea of

---

[20] "Orthodox, traditional Christianity is so firmly rooted in Hellenistic antiquity that many Christian thinkers, ancient and recent, rather naturally bolstered biblical doctrines with arguments from classical pagan thought, and later, from modern rationalist thought, especially German idealism. Often they altered the Bible's teachings in the process, as they called these philosophical arguments into service to reinforce Christian convictions. Plato, Cicero, and later thinkers such as the philosopher M. Mendelssohn and the mathematician G.W. Leibniz argued, as we have noted, that the soul, as a simple substance, cannot decompose and therefore must be immortal." Harold O.J. Brown, "Will the Lost Suffer Forever", *Criswell Theological Review* 4 (1990): 275.

[21] Robert A. Peterson, *Hell on Trial: The Case for Eternal Punishment* (Phillipsburg: P & R Publishing, 1995) 178.

an immortal soul, the criticisms of this doctrine to follow will not apply to all traditionalists equally. Some traditionalists will even agree with some of the criticisms. The primary goal is to clarify the biblical meaning of immortality and to show that the traditional idea really creates more problems than it solves.

The Meaning of Immortality

When speaking of immortality, the Bible always speaks in reference to God and the redeemed. Several passages prove this, the most important being 1 Timothy 6:15b-16:

> God, the blessed and only Ruler, the King of kings and Lord of lords, who alone is immortal and who lives in unapproachable light, whom no one has seen or can see. To him be honor and might forever. Amen.

Paul says that God alone is immortal. Since other passages speak of the immortality of the redeemed (1 Cor. 15:53), the apostle must mean that God is immortal in some way that even the redeemed are not. The main difference between God and mankind according to the Bible is that God is uncreated and mankind is created. In other words, God has no beginning and lives forever, but mankind has a beginning and can live forever. God's life, then, is underived and independent; our life is derived and dependent. Therefore, it is correct to say that God alone has immortality because only God is immortal by nature.

In the New Testament, two Greek words are used for immortality: *athanasia* and *aphtharsia*. D.W. Kerr explains their usage in the New Testament:

> **Athanasia** is the exact equivalent of the English immortality, as it is used in 1 Cor. 15:53-54 where it describes the resurrection body as one which is not subject to death; and in 1 Tim. 6:16 where God is said to be the one who alone has immortality. He alone in his essence is deathless. **Aphtharsia** has the basic meaning of indestructibility and, by derivation, of incorruption, by which it is rendered in the familiar resurrection paean in 1 Cor. 15:42ff. in the AV. The translation ***immortality*** is used, however, in Rom. 2:7, where the reference is to the life of glory and honor to which the believer aspires; in II Tim. 1:10, where it is said that Christ "abolished death and brought life and ***immortality*** to light." The adjective **aphthartos** is used to describe God as not being subject to diminution or decay (Rom. 1:23; 1 Tim. 1:17); or of things which are not perishable, such as the crown awarded to the successful Christian (1 Cor. 9:25), the inheritance which is reserved for the Christian (1 Pet. 1:4), the seed of which the Christian is born (1 Pet. 1:23).[22]

Kerr summarizes these usages by saying "that immortality in the biblical sense is a condition in which the individual is not subject to death or any other influence which might lead to death."[23] Clearly, the traditional

---

[22] D. W. Kerr, "Immortality", *Evangelical Dictionary of Theology*, ed. Walter A. Elwell (Grand Rapids: Baker Book House, 1984) 551.

[23] Kerr 551-552.

concept of an immortal soul does not fit the biblical data. Mankind is not inherently immortal but immortal only in Christ. As Paul says, Christ "has destroyed death and has brought life and immortality to light through the gospel." (2 Tim. 1:10) Also, the immortal person in Christ is not simply an immortal soul—the entire person receives immortality.[24] The first point is made especially clear in Romans 2:7: "To those who by persistence in doing good *seek* glory, honor and immortality, he will give eternal life." If immortality is a natural endowment of the soul, then there would be no need to seek it. The second point is made in 1 Corinthians 15:54:

> For the perishable must clothe itself with the imperishable, and the mortal with immortality. When the perishable has been clothed with the imperishable, and the mortal with immortality, then the saying that is written will come true: "Death has been swallowed up in victory."

Given these passages, it is amazing that the Christian Church would develop the doctrine of the immortality of the soul. Even if God were to sustain the conscious existence of the damned in hell, there would be no reason, biblically speaking, to refer to them as "immortal souls," for even traditionalists believe that the lost suffer in both body and soul. These facts explain why many critics of the traditional

---

[24] Kerr 552.

view believe that the doctrine of immortal soulism came from Plato and not the Bible.[25]

The most glaring inconsistency with the biblical usage, however, is that the damned are referred to as immortal. How can a word that means deathlessness and incorruption refer to a person who is supposedly dying forever and undergoing eternal corruption? This is not simply a paradox—it is an oxymoron! According to the traditional view, the lost are forever dead being alive, forever corrupted being incorruptible—in both body and soul![26] Surely terms that denote deathlessness and incorruption should not be used in reference to those outside of Christ.

Perhaps the clearest evidence that God did not create mankind immortal is provided in Genesis 3:22. Traditionalists often assume that each person has an immortal soul because of the image of God. Supposedly, "the very fact that humanity was created in such a way as to be able to enjoy a living relationship with an immortal God is at least a hint that he was created in the same 'dimension.'"[27] This kind of argument is so weak that it is amazing that it has been put forth. Why should the image confer God's immortality on mankind but not his

---

[25] Clark Pinnock, "Fire, Then Nothing", *Christianity Today* 20 Mar. 1987: 40-41.

[26] The damned cannot be compared to those Paul calls "dead in transgressions and sins" (Eph. 2:1). The dead in sins are physically alive and spiritually dead, but according to the traditionalist, the damned are dead in both senses and yet forever conscious. Obviously, the concepts of life and death are being defined in a very restricted sense by traditionalists.

[27] John Blanchard, *Whatever Happened to Hell?* (Wheaton: Crossway Books, 1995) 215.

omniscience? Genesis 3:22 shows that the image of God does not even provide a hint of natural immortality:

> And the LORD God said, "The man has now become like one of us, knowing good and evil. He must not be allowed to reach out his hand and take also from the tree of life and eat, and live forever."

This verse says something that is often overlooked in the biblical record. Adam and Eve were dependent on the tree of life before they fell and could have continued to live without death even after they fell. In other words, the tree of life, not some immortal quality, was responsible for the sustenance of their earthy lives. This verse is a powerful testimony to the fact that mankind was created mortal and avoided death only by continued fellowship with God, which gave them the right to the life-giving qualities of the sacred tree.

Traditionalists are quick to point out that the death suffered by Adam and Eve was a spiritual death, not a physical death, for God said, "when you eat of it you will surely die." (Gen. 2:17) Since the death experienced through the fall was a spiritual death, they argue, we should understand death as separation from God and eternal death as eternal separation from God. In this way, the idea of the dissolution of the body does not need to have any affect on our understanding of final punishment. This sounds good at first glance, but the physical dimension of death is also involved in the penalty for sin and therefore is involved in our understanding of final punishment in the Bible. Death is both separation from God and the eventual dissolution of the entire person. In barring Adam and Eve from the tree of life, God showed that the sentence of eventual physical death was as much a part of the penalty for sin as immediate spiritual death. But more on this later.

The key question can now be answered: Is man's soul of such a nature that even the fires of hell cannot destroy it? On the basis of the biblical evidence, a negative answer must be given. This is not to say that God is unable to sustain the existence of a person for all eternity if it were his will to do so. It is only to say that there is nothing within the constitution of mankind that requires it. While this does not prove the doctrine of conditional immortality, it certainly clears away some of the traditional clutter obscuring a better view of the biblical teaching about final punishment.

The Case for Natural Immortality

With this orientation to the issue, it will be helpful to review some of the arguments that have been put forth in support of the idea of natural immortality.[28] There are seven arguments worth considering, one of which is referenced above. In looking at each one, it is helpful to determine precisely what it proves, if anything. What may come as a surprise is that competent Christian theologians have put these arguments forth as proofs for natural

---

[28] James A. Nichols, *Christian Doctrines* (Nutley: The Craig Press, 1970) 126-128.

immortality, even though many theologians today, including traditionalists, would never resort to them.[29]

Argument One: The soul is by nature indestructible because it is simple (has no parts). If the soul has no parts, it cannot die because death involves a dissolution, or falling apart. This is obviously a philosophical argument with a number of problems. First of all, how can it be known that the soul is simple and has no parts? And furthermore, must the soul be separated in order to die? Jesus says that God is able to destroy the soul in hell (Mt. 10:28), so why is God unable to destroy a simple soul? Is anything too hard for God?

Argument Two: Because we never fulfill ourselves or our purpose in this life, the soul must be eternal. As W.G.T. Shedd writes, "Every spiritual desire and aspiration has in it the element of infinity and endlessness."[30] This argument proves nothing more than that some human beings have aspirations that cannot be realized in one lifetime. It does not prove that any or all must live forever. Ecclesiastes 3:11 says that God has set eternity in our hearts; it does not say that this guarantees eternal existence to any. The Bible does, however, speak of eternal life for those in Christ. According to the Bible, then, any eternal aspirations people may have are only fulfilled in Christ.

Argument Three: People are not adequately punished in this life for their evil deeds; therefore, justice must come

---

[29] cf. Brown 274-276. Harold Brown, a traditionalist, surveys many of the following arguments and admits that they are simply not compelling.

[30] W.G.T. Shedd, *The Doctrine of Endless Punishment* (Carlisle: Banner of Truth Trust, 1990) 51.

in the next. This argument makes a very powerful appeal for a final judgment and punishment of sin, but it certainly does not prove the need for an immortal soul or eternal torment. When this argument is used as a basis for eternal torment, it simply begs the question of how long the punishment must last. There is no good reason why the penal suffering and ultimate destruction of sinners cannot satisfy ultimate justice as well as endless punishing.[31]

Argument Four: All nations and ages have a concept of immortality; therefore, each person has an immortal soul. Like argument two, this one simply cannot go the distance. Even if all nations have a concept of immortality, this does not mean that God has created us with immortal souls. According to the Bible, even eternal aspirations can be frustrated by sin. An eternal aspiration does not prove an eternal constitution.

Argument Five: The soul is immortal because mankind is made in God's image, and God is immortal. The major problem with this argument is that it attempts to connect immortality to the image of God in mankind. This is a false connection, as the previous discussion of immortality demonstrates. Immortality in the Bible is connected to Christ, not to the image of God. Even the image itself, which is marred by sin, is restored only in Christ. If immortality were connected to the image of God, we

---

[31] Traditionalists will argue, of course, that there is a reason why ultimate destruction cannot satisfy God's justice as well as endless punishing. They believe that finite sins incur an infinite debt of guilt that requires an endless punishing. As the next chapter will show, this is a reason to believe as they do, but it is not a good reason because it is not biblical.

should logically figure that it was lost in the fall and had to be restored in Christ, given everything the New Testament says about life in Christ.

Argument Six: Because hell is eternal, the soul must be immortal to survive the punishment. Of all seven arguments, this is the only one that is common to all traditionalists. It is a good argument, of course, only if the Bible actually teaches endless punishing. As mentioned earlier, however, it still fails to use the correct term for the eternal existence of the damned.[32] Their souls and bodies live forever if punishment lasts forever, not just their souls. Also, there is no way, biblically speaking, that the term *immortal* can apply to them. Again, the biblical terms denote deathlessness and incorruption, not eternal death and corruption.

Argument Seven: The Pharisees believed in the immortality of the soul and endless torment. Since Jesus and Paul came from this background and never explicitly denied these teachings, they must have believed them.[33] While this sounds like a good argument, it is really fallacious. It is, in fact, an argument from silence. In other words, a person can be assumed to believe whatever he does not explicitly deny. If this were the case, we could all be pegged with beliefs we were associated with but simply never disavowed publicly. This argument also overlooks the

---

[32] It is interesting to think about what term would be a good substitute to describe what traditionalists really believe. Instead of the immortality of the soul, *the eternity of the self* would be much more accurate.

[33] William Crockett, *Four Views on Hell*, ed. William Crockett (Grand Rapids: Zondervan Publishing House, 1992) 68ff.

many other Pharisaical beliefs that neither Jesus nor Paul openly rejected. Edward Fudge summarizes this argument and gives an apt response to it:

> Thus traditionalist writers have frequently assumed that by his relative silence Jesus endorsed the Pharisees' belief in the immortality of the soul. Jewish thought of Jesus' time is then represented as having only two strains - outright Platonic dualism (held by the Pharisees) and utter materialism (held by the Sadducees). Since the Gospel's record Jesus' rejection of the Sadducees' doctrine, it is assumed that he agreed with the Pharisees. Such reasoning overlooks the diversity of Jewish thought illustrated in the sources. It also proves more than orthodox theologians would wish to affirm since Josephus may indicate a Pharisaic belief in the transmigration of souls.[34]

In looking at the arguments for the natural immortality of the soul, one is astounded by the words of W.G.T. Shedd, whose book on endless punishment is the classic defense of the traditional position: "But this doctrine [the immortality of the soul], like that of Divine existence, is nowhere formally demonstrated, because it is everywhere assumed."[35] After looking at the Bible and the traditional arguments, most will conclude that the only place natural immortality is "everywhere assumed" is in the minds of the traditional theologians who espouse it. Unfortunately,

---

[34] Edward William Fudge, *The Fire That Consumes* (Carlisle UK: Paternoster Press, 1994) 27n.

[35] Shedd 51.

many Protestants and Roman Catholics take the doctrine for granted because it has been touted as an obvious tenet of orthodoxy for so long. For many, the belief that God created the soul immortal drives their commitment to endless torment and colors their view of biblical language more than they realize. Therefore, it is time to clear away this theological error so that discussion about the duration of hell may proceed without hindrance.

The Case for Openness

The zeal with which this false doctrine has been advocated in history should teach Christians something about the psychology of belief. Christians are often far too credulous when it comes to things they want to believe, so credulous, in fact, that they will resort to flimsy arguments that clearly depart from the language of the Bible. Traditionalists often accuse conditionalists of rejecting endless punishing simply because they want to believe something more palatable. Conditionalists are often accused of departing from the plain language of the Bible because of a "sentimental" attitude about final punishment. Those who make such accusations rarely look at their own feelings to see if, in fact, they have an emotional agenda that is leading them to overlook the consumption and destruction language of the Bible.

The truth is that some traditionalists are often quite closed-minded and fearful of any position other than endless torment, and this leads them to ignore and distort biblical evidence. Many traditionalists have been taught that any compromise on the doctrine of endless punishing is the beginning of a short slide down the slippery slope to liberalism and unbelief.[36] In a desperate attempt to guard the fortress of orthodoxy at all costs, some will resort to any argument, including the ones refuted above, in order to "defend the faith." The desire to defend the faith is a reflection of sincerity toward God and is commendable. But this sincerity may also be a cover for a kind of emotional pollution traditionalists see in others but not in themselves.

Many traditionalists are fearful about losing the traditional view of hell because that would mean that much of the Church has been wrong about hell for centuries. Despite the fact that the Protestant belief in justification by faith apart from meritorious works was a minority view

[36] The extent to which fear and closed-mindedness can take hold of Christians was brought home to me in a personal letter from Dr. Gary North. I had written to him with a series of questions challenging the exegesis behind the traditional position. I had sent these questions to several other well-known evangelical scholars for a response, but only one has responded besides Dr. North. The following excerpt from his letter demonstrates how hyperorthodox zeal is often used to avoid dealing with biblical issues: "I am not about to dilly-dally with anyone who espouses it [conditional immortality]. I would as willingly spend time debating the Trinity. Some theological topics are beyond debate; they are better used to conduct heresy trials. The doctrine of hell is one of them. I will put it bluntly: you are a heretic. I suggest that you get your thinking straight before you apostatize. But it is not my task to do this for you; any Protestant systematic theology will serve as a surrogate for me." Gary North, letter to the author, 4 Aug. 1995. This response is quite the opposite of the one I received from Dr. John Piper. Instead of calling me a heretic, Dr. Piper expressed his disagreement this way: "I pray that the Lord will lead us into truth for the sake of his desperately needy Bride and for the sake of what I think is a world perishing a much more horrible fate than you apparently do." John Piper, letter to the author, 6 Jan. 1996. In addition to a very charitable attitude, Dr. Piper also expressed a willingness to continue discussion on the subject.

until the early 1500's, many evangelicals are stubborn when it comes to hell. There are two reasons for this.

First, many feel that if the Church has been wrong about hell, then the Holy Spirit has not led the Church into all truth. Many Christians take Jesus' promise in John 16:13 as a guarantee that the established theology of the Church must be right: "But when he, the Spirit of truth, comes, he will guide you into all truth. He will not speak on his own; he will speak only what he hears, and he will tell you what is yet to come." This promise, however, was made to the disciples, not to the entire Church after the apostles. If this promise is taken to apply to the Church throughout history, then the Spirit obviously failed because there has never been a monolithic Christian theology, despite what the Roman and Eastern Orthodox Churches may preach. The real evidence of the Spirit's work throughout history is the Church's progress in biblical understanding, not its static formulations that prove themselves unbiblical over time. Protestants who jealously guard the doctrine of eternal torment because it is historical need to reconsider their understanding of the Spirit's work in the Church.[37]

Second, many feel that departures from the traditional view of hell will lead to departures in other areas of doctrine. Since even traditionalists find endless torment difficult to swallow, it should be no surprise to them that liberal attacks

---

[37] They should also reconsider what is at the heart of their assurance that the Christian faith is true. What do they trust most: The Bible or the Church's interpretation of it?

on the Bible generally begin here. Liberalism, however, represents a rejection of biblical authority. Evangelical conditionalists do not reject biblical authority and believe that all doctrinal formulations must be consistent with the Bible. Unfortunately, the fears of many traditionalists in this area are not informed by a clear understanding of liberalism. A rationalistic approach to the Bible will always lead to progressive defections from plain biblical teachings. Historically, evangelicals have been very rationalistic in their thinking, which is why liberalism develops within conservative denominations. Hyperorthodoxy, rationalism, and bad theological arguments—all provoke reactions. The fact that some rationalists have rejected the traditional view just because they do not like it does not prove that all challenges to it are so motivated. People question things for different reasons, and sometimes there are very good reasons to question traditional beliefs.

The doctrine of the immortality of the soul is a good example of a long standing belief that is bogus and worthy of rejection. Conservatives must beware of knee-jerk reactions to those who question their cherished beliefs. If a belief is biblical, it will stand up to stringent criticism and careful cross-examination. The doctrine of the immortality of the soul does not pass the biblical test and should be thrown on the theological trash heap of history. As long as the Bible passes the verdict and not autonomous creatures, we should welcome the liberation that comes from progressing to a better understanding of truth.

Chapter 2
FAVORITE ARGUMENTS FOR ENDLESS TORMENT

It should now be clear that traditionalists should not use the term *the immortality of the soul* at all but should speak instead of *the eternity of the self*. This serves to remove the excess clutter from the discussion about final punishment and allows everyone to concentrate on their main point: Hell is forever, so the self must be eternal in order to survive the punishment. This focuses the discussion on the most important question: Is hell forever? The eternity of the self, then, is really just an implication of the traditional position; it is not an argument for it.

Traditionalists have been too hasty in claiming that the Bible obviously supports their belief. They quote many verses that they think are clear in teaching the endless punishing of those outside of Christ. What they do not quote is the conditionalist authors who challenge their supposedly obvious interpretations and the many assumptions behind them. In fact, it is amazing that in many recent books defending the traditional position, not one that I have consulted attempts to interact with the manner in which conditionalists treat all the major verses on the subject.[38] By examining the major arguments used by traditionalists, endless torment may not appear as obvious as it once did.

Eternal Guilt Requires Eternal Hell

The key assumption behind the traditional view is that finite sins incur infinite guilt before God that requires an endless, conscious torment. Like the belief in an immortal soul, this principle has become such a truism that most people read it into the pages of the Bible instead of reading it out. Several arguments are put forth, some biblical and some theological. The biblical arguments will be surveyed first.

---

[38] The recent book by Robert Peterson is a good example. Peterson interacts with conditionalist interpretations of Revelation 14:11 and 20:10 but says little about other passages in question. This is a common pattern in the current literature. The reason for this may be that most of the well-known conditionalists do not do an adequate job in dealing with these passages, so it is in the traditionalist's favor to interact with their exegesis of these verses. On other verses, traditionalists do not seem as eager to interact with conditionalist interpretations. Rather than telling their readers how conditionalists handle a particular verse and then refuting them, they simply give their own interpretation as the obvious one. The net effect is that the reader doesn't know anything more about how different passages are interpreted than he knew at the start. In reality, traditionalist authors often mislead their readers into seeing only what they want them to see by not showing them any alternatives or by not presenting alternatives accurately. This is a common tactic used by salespeople and advertisers. Unfortunately, Christian scholars occasionally succumb to this temptation, even though they are generally fair. As far as the two previously mentioned verses in Revelation are concerned, the next chapter will deal with those in detail.

Matthew 12:31-32 is often used in support of the idea of infinite guilt:

> 31 And so I tell you, every sin and blasphemy will be forgiven men, but the blasphemy against the Spirit will not be forgiven. 32 Anyone who speaks a word against the Son of Man will be forgiven, but anyone who speaks against the Holy Spirit will not be forgiven, either in this age or in the age to come.

The traditional argument from these verses is simple: "Not forgiven" means never forgiven, because this age and the age to come covers both time and eternity; this means that the unforgiven are eternally guilty; therefore, the lost must exist forever because their guilt lasts forever.[39] This argument sounds plausible, but it contains a major assumption. Traditionalists are smuggling the idea of conscious existence into these verses when the words of Jesus do not require it. The fact that a person is never forgiven does not require that the person exist forever. Conditionalists agree with these verses too, which is why they believe that once a person is punished and destroyed, he will never be forgiven by God or brought back to life.[40]

Traditionalists are habituated in the belief that the unforgiven person must exist in order for eternal unforgiveness to have any meaning. Therefore, an example from the Old Testament will illustrate why eternal existence need not be assumed. Isaiah 66:24 refers to the dead bodies

---
[39] Leon Morris, "Eternal Punishment", *Evangelical Dictionary of Theology* 369.
[40] Conditionalists believe in eternal consequences for sin, not infinite guilt.

of those who rebelled against the Lord:

> 24 "And they will go out and look upon the dead bodies of those who rebelled against me; their worm will not die, nor will their fire be quenched, and they will be loathsome to all mankind."

Here is a picture of dead bodies being destroyed by fire and eaten by worms. Even though these are corpses and therefore not alive and conscious, Isaiah says *they* will be loathsome to all mankind.[41] In short, it is possible to loath someone who is no longer alive. Hitler, for example, will be the object of loathing forever, even though he is nowhere to be found alive and well. Because he once existed as a person, we can loath his memory. Similarly, those who are destroyed can be spoken of as "never forgiven", even though they do not continue to exist as conscious persons. Because they are never forgiven, they are forever destroyed.

The assumption of infinite guilt is being smuggled into Jesus' words by riding piggyback on the assumption of eternal existence. But does not Jesus also say in Matthew 3:29 that everyone who blasphemes against the Holy Spirit is guilty of an eternal sin? Surely this proves that someone is eternally guilty and must, therefore, exist forever. This argument overlooks that fact that the eternal sin may simply produce eternal consequences. Obviously, the sin itself is not being committed eternally; it is committed in time and is not ongoing. It makes more sense to view Jesus'

---

[41] See the discussion of the undying worms and unquenchable fire below.

words as a statement of consequences for the sin. Viewed this way, conditionalists affirm that blaspheming the Holy Spirit does have eternal consequences, but those consequences in no way require the eternal existence of those guilty of the sin.

Matthew 5:25-26 is also used to argue for an infinite debt of sin that requires endless torment:

> 25 "Settle matters quickly with your adversary who is taking you to court. Do it while you are still with him on the way, or he may hand you over to the judge, and the judge may hand you over to the officer, and you may be thrown into prison. 26 I tell you the truth, you will not get out until you have paid the last penny."

John Blanchard summarizes the argument made from these verses: "Jesus taught that the person sent to hell's prison would not get out until he had paid 'the last penny' (Matthew 5:26), the inescapable inference being that the last penny can never be paid."[42] The inference of this argument is "inescapable," as Blanchard says, but his conclusion of endless torment is not. A debtor might not be released from prison while he is alive, but once he dies, he will certainly be removed from the prison. In fact, these verses support conditional immortality, not the traditional view. The lost do not escape from the prison of hell alive! This, it would seem, is the logical conclusion of Jesus' words. This argument is a good example of another case

---

[42] Blanchard 223.

where the assumption of conscious existence is smuggled into the text. So powerful is the assumption that traditionalists do not even see that their own argument really works against their position.

The problem for the traditionalist is that the Bible simply does not teach that finite sins require an infinite punishment. As an example of how unbiblical assumptions blind Christians to what the Bible says, consider Luke 12:47-48, a major passage on God's distributive justice:

> 47 "That servant who knows his master's will and does not get ready or does not do what his master wants will be beaten with many blows. 48 But the one who does not know and does things deserving punishment will be beaten with few blows. From everyone who has been given much, much will be demanded; and from the one who has been entrusted with much, much more will be asked."

These verses hardly teach the idea of infinite punishment for finite sin. In fact, they teach the same principle developed in the Law of Moses (Ex. 21:23-25; Deut. 25:2-3). Ironically, traditionalists quote this passage as evidence that there will be degrees of punishment in hell. They assume, however, that hell's torments will be infinite in duration but finite in severity.[43] A little reflection on this distinction in light of the principle of infinite guilt shows it to be incoherent. If every sin incurs infinite or limitless guilt, then how can there be degrees of punishment

---
[43] Crockett 73.

at all? The principle of infinite guilt requires infinite punishing for each and every sin. In other words, since every sin incurs infinite guilt, it is impossible to distinguish between more and less aggravated sins. Adding two infinites together does not give you a double infinite, does it? And yet, this is precisely what the traditional view of infinite guilt requires in order to support a distinction between infinite duration and finite severity. That such a distinction would even be offered as intelligible shows a lack of self-criticism among traditionalists when it comes to hell.

Surprisingly, traditionalists accuse conditionalists of not being able to accommodate Jesus' teaching on degrees of punishment. First, they misrepresent conditionalists by characterizing them all as simple annihilationists.[44] The simple annihilationist believes that there is no period of penal suffering in hell before the sinner is destroyed.[45] Most conditionalists do not believe this, and it is unscholarly and unfair to use such tactics. Most conditionalists believe in degrees of punishment precisely because of what Jesus and the Old Testament say about differing degrees of guilt for sin.

The traditionalist really cannot support his case using Luke 12:47-48. How is it that Jesus refers to degrees of punishment as "few" and "many" stripes—a finite number of stripes—when traditionalists say that all sinners receive an infinite number of stripes in hell? On the logic of endless torment, Jesus should have spoken of light and heavy

---

[44] See Crockett 73, Blanchard 67-68.

[45] Jehovah's Witnesses are simple annihilationists.

stripes, since the stripes never end. An infinite number of stripes simply makes nonsense out of Jesus' words.

Also, how do we explain the fact that Deuteronomy 25:2-3 forbids excessive punishment because it is degrading if, as traditionalists say, hell has no limits?

> 2 If the guilty man deserves to be beaten, the judge shall make him lie down and have him flogged in his presence with the number of lashes his crime deserves, 3 but he must not give him more than forty lashes. If he is flogged more than that, your brother will be degraded in your eyes.

According to the traditional view, God violates the principle of his own law by punishing sinners in hell forever, making them truly degraded and insignificant. Some will argue that the Law of Moses only reflects principles for human justice:

> Earthly courts and judges look at the transgression of law with reference only to man's temporal relations, not his eternal. They punish an offence as a crime against the State, not as a sin against God.[46]

Shedd goes on to say that human judges lack the omniscience of God, which prevents them from seeing the "sum-total of guilt in the case."[47] This is why they can only punish sin in a limited way. Shedd clearly recognizes that the Old Testament presents a principle of guilt and punishment

---

[46] Shedd 132.
[47] Shedd 133.

that contradicts his belief in the infinite guilt of sin. Therefore, he must find some way to justify the Bible's use of two opposite principles. It is totally arbitrary and mistaken to assume, as he does, that the Old Testament reckons offenses as crimes against the state only. In Israel, all crimes against the state were also crimes against God. In the Bible, the civil magistrate is God's "agent of wrath to bring punishment on the wrongdoer." (Rom. 13:4) His contention that human judges can only punish sin in a limited way because they lack God's omniscience is simply ludicrous. In fact, a lack of omniscience does *not* keep us from seeing the sum-total of guilt in the case since, according to Shedd, the Bible tells us that all sins incur infinite guilt. We know exactly what the sum-total of guilt is in every case! Shedd simply fails to account for the discrepancy between the Old Testament's view of guilt and punishment and his own. Interestingly, Luke 12:47-48 is directly in line with Deuteronomy 25:2-3, speaking as it does of few and many stripes.

There is also an important theological argument that is often made to justify the notion of infinite guilt. Shedd makes the argument that the incarnation and vicarious atonement of the second person of the Godhead proves that the guilt of sin is infinite:

> The incarnation and vicarious satisfaction for sin by one of the persons of the Godhead, demonstrates the infinity of the evil. It is incredible that the Eternal Trinity should have submitted to such a stupendous self-sacrifice, to

remove a merely finite and temporal evil. The doctrine of Christ's vicarious atonement, logically, stands or falls with that of endless punishment. Historically, it has stood or fallen with it. The incarnation of Almighty God, in order to make the remission of sin possible, is one of the strongest arguments for the eternity and infinity of penal suffering.[48]

This argument sounds impressive, but it really plays on the ignorance of those who are not familiar with the biblical reasons why God became a man in the person of Jesus Christ. Shedd leads readers to think that there is only one reason why God had to become a man, and that is because sin is so infinitely heinous that only God could remove it. This is another case of reading a presupposition into the Bible, since the Bible nowhere says that God had to become a man because of the infinite guilt of sin. Christ's role as Mediator and High Priest required the incarnation because, as a Mediator, Christ had to represent both God and mankind (Heb. 2:14-18). Perhaps the most important reason God had to become human is that throughout the Bible God proclaims himself the Savior of mankind:

> 9 Help us, O God our Savior, for the glory of your name; deliver us and forgive our sins for your name's sake. (Ps. 79:9)

These reasons for the incarnation and atonement show that there is not just one reason why God had to become

---

[48] Shedd 153.

human. The infinite value of Christ's death does play a part in his atonement, but not the part Shedd assigns to it. The infinite value of Christ's death shows that there is no quantity of sin that can ever exhaust its value, and there was no need for Christ to suffer on the cross beyond a few hours to make atonement for our sins.[49] When Shedd says that the incarnation and vicarious atonement stand or fall with the doctrine of eternal torment, he is using scare tactics. The countless passages that proclaim God the Savior of mankind explain the necessity for the incarnation and atonement of Christ. One need not posit infinite guilt just to insure the safety of these doctrines.

Eternal Fire Requires Eternal Hell

The most familiar argument for endless torment is based on the passages in the New Testament that speak of "unquenchable fire." The purpose of the fires of hell, according to traditionalists is to torment, not to consume.[50] They must argue this way because, in their view, sinners are never actually burned up by the fire but are eternally conscious of their sufferings. Perhaps the strongest language

---

[49] The short period of time Christ suffered on the cross really argues for the principle of finite guilt. As God, he simply didn't need to suffer very long to take away our sins.

[50] Many traditionalists do not take the imagery of hell literally, because hell is often spoken of as both "fire" and "outer darkness." Since fire produces light and not darkness, it seems that the images were not meant to be taken literally. This does not mean that they do not give a meaningful description of what hell will be like. For an excellent defense of the metaphorical view of the biblical language about hell, see Crockett 43-61.

Jesus ever used to describe hell is found in Mark 9:47-48:

> 47 And if your eye causes you to sin, pluck it out. It is better for you to enter the kingdom of God with one eye than to have two eyes and be thrown into hell, 48 where "'their worm does not die, and the fire is not quenched.'"

On the surface, it is not difficult to see why both Christians and non-Christians have understood this language in terms of endless torment. A fire that is not quenched certainly sounds like an ever-burning fire, and why would the worms be called undying unless there would always be something available to eat? The problem is that this is not the only way to understand the language. Jesus is taking his imagery from a garbage dump outside of Jerusalem, which is evident by his use of the word *gehenna* for hell. The background of this word is important in understanding why Jesus used it:

> The word Gehenna is the Greek equivalent for "the valley of Hinnom" (Josh. 15:8; 18:16; Neh. 11:30). It thus originally referred to the Valley of Hinnom, which was just outside the city of Jerusalem. According to ***Thayer's Greek-English Lexicon*** (p. 111), it was the place where idolatrous Jews gave human sacrifices to pagan deities (2 Kings 23:10; 2 Chron. 28:3; 33:6). Because of these horrible practices, the Valley of Hinnom was hated and considered "unclean" by Jews. In Christ's day, this hatred of the Valley of Hinnom caused the valley to become the town dump where all the garbage of Jerusalem could be thrown into it. Because garbage was constantly being

thrown into the valley, the fires never stopped burning and the worms never stopped eating.[51]

It is interesting to compare the different uses made of this imagery by both traditionalists and conditionalists. Traditionalists emphasize the fact that "the fires never stopped burning and the worms never stopped eating." This suggests to them that Jesus meant to teach that people will consciously suffer forever without being destroyed. Conditionalists, on the other hand, point out that the worms and fire consume the refuse. This suggests to them that Jesus meant to teach that people will be consumed by the ever-present worms and fire, not that they will be eaten and burned alive forever.

The conditionalist use of the imagery certainly makes more sense than the traditionalist use, since it is difficult to conceive how a person could be continuously eaten by worms and burned with fire and yet not consumed.[52] Traditionalists, of course will simply affirm that the consumption aspect of the imagery was never meant to inform our view of Jesus' meaning. How do they know this? Their answer is that the fire of hell is spoken of as "eternal" and the worms are "undying," so Jesus did not intend to reinforce this part of the imagery.

---

[51] Morey 87.

[52] Some traditionalists will point to the burning bush (Ex. 3:2) as an example of something that was on fire but did not burn up. This example is not relevant to the language about hell, since the New Testament speaks of the fire of hell as a consuming fire (Mt. 3:12; Heb. 10:27).

The truth, however, is that he did intend to reinforce these aspects. We know this because the Bible provides clear counterexamples to show us that an unquenchable fire is a fire that cannot be stopped; it is not a fire that never stops. Consider the following passages:

> 27 But if you do not obey me to keep the Sabbath day holy by not carrying any load as you come through the gates of Jerusalem on the Sabbath day, then I will kindle an unquenchable fire in the gates of Jerusalem that will consume her fortresses.'" (Jer. 17:27)

> 7 In a similar way, Sodom and Gomorrah and the surrounding towns gave themselves up to sexual immorality and perversion. They serve as an example of those who suffer the punishment of eternal fire. (Jude 7)

The passage from Jeremiah records a threat to the inhabitants of Jerusalem for Sabbath breaking. This threat was carried out by God when the Babylonians sacked Jerusalem in 586 B.C. and burned the city and its gates with fire. How interesting that God would refer to a temporary fire that eventually burned out as an "unquenchable fire"! Obviously unquenchable fires in the Bible are not fires that never stop—they are fires that cannot be stopped.

The passage from Jude describes the destruction of Sodom and Gomorrah. These wicked cities of the plain were destroyed by what Jude here calls an "eternal fire." Phillip Hughes points out that the word *eternal* can have a qualitative as well as a quantitative meaning. In other words, the word *eternal* does not always refer to an infinite quantity of time. Hughes explains:

> Even though this was not the final judgment, the obliterating fire is described as *eternal* fire, the fire of judgment sent by the Lord; for obviously in the case of these cities the fire was not eternally endured by their inhabitants. It was fire that struck and left devastation from which no restoration could follow.[53]

Traditionalists will argue with this interpretation for a couple of reasons. Some will dogmatically state that the word *eternal* refers to time only and never to the quality of an object.[54] This must be proven by all the occurrences of the word in the Bible, which do not bear out this contention. John's use of the phrase "eternal life" throughout his gospel clearly stresses the quality of the life as well as the quantity or duration of life in Christ.

Others will argue that a verb tense in Jude 7 contradicts the conditionalist interpretation. Jude says that the inhabitants of Sodom and Gommorah serve as an example of those who *suffer* (present tense) the punishment of eternal fire. To put it more emphatically—those who *are suffering* the punishment of eternal fire. First of all, it is difficult to see how those who were terminated by a

---

[53] Phillip Edgcumbe Hughes, *The True Image: The Origin and Destiny of Man in Christ* (Grand Rapids: Wm. B. Eerdmans Publishing Co., 1989) 402.

[54] Shedd 87.

temporary fire can be an example of those who are suffering an eternal fire. After all, the inhabitants of Sodom and Gomorrah were consumed, but the inhabitants of hell are never consumed according to the traditional view. In fact, Jude is not attempting to compare the inhabitants of Sodom and Gommorah with the inhabitants of hell at all. He is telling his readers what these people are, namely, examples of those who suffer the punishment of eternal fire.

The intent of Jude's language may be illustrated by using a parallel sentence. Consider the following: General Patton is a good example of those who fight for their country. In this sentence, the word *fight* merely serves to define the subject (General Patton) as a member of a class (those who fight). In doing so, the word *fight* has no reference to a battle taking place in the present. In other words, the class of those who fight is really an abstract group; it is not made up of a specific person or persons currently engaged in battle. The purpose of this construction is to explain the meaning of the idea of fighting for one's country by using a familiar example. Because of this, it would be a mistake to think of General Patton as himself presently fighting or as an example of others presently fighting. Jude's use of the word *suffer* has the same purpose and grammar as my example, and the NIV translators wisely made this clear in the translation. The destruction of the inhabitants of Sodom and Gommorah explains the meaning of the idea of suffering the punishment of eternal fire. A simple paraphrase may help to clarify Jude's point:

Look at what happened to the people of Sodom and Gommorah—that is what it means to be punished by an eternal fire. Two things are evident, then, from this interpretation: (1) Jude is not comparing the inhabitants of Sodom and Gommorah to those presently suffering endless torment in hell; (2) Jude had no intention of communicating the idea that an eternal fire is an endless fire that torments the lost forever.[55]

In light of what has been said, the traditional belief that unquenchable and eternal fires must last forever is simply not accurate, and the Bible itself proves it by clear counterexamples. These examples are there for traditionalists to see, but they never seem to notice them. Could it be that the reason for this is that traditionalists are simply habituated in a belief that keeps them from seeing things differently? One wonders when very good theologians like Anthony Hoekema cannot seem to see another way to look at the language of unquenchable fire and undying worms. His comment on Mark 9:43 is typical of most traditionalists: "If the figures used in this passage do not mean unending suffering, they mean nothing at all."[56] Hoekema's argument

---

[55] For those interested in consulting the original language on this point, consider Burton's explanation of a common use of the present active participle in the New Testament: "The General Present Participle. The Present Participle is also used without reference to time or progress, simply defining its subject as belonging to a certain class, *i.e.* the class of those who do the action denoted by the verb. The participle in this case becomes a simple adjective or noun and is, like any other adjective or noun, timeless and indefinite." Ernest De Witt Burton, *Syntax of the Moods and Tenses in New Testament Greek* (Grand Rapids: Kregal Publications, 1994) 56.

[56] Anthony A. Hoekema, *The Bible and the Future* (Grand Rapids: Wm. B. Eerdmans, 1978) 268.

commits the false alternative fallacy because he excludes a viable option without adequate justification.

Eternal Life Requires Eternal Hell

Another favorite argument for endless torment is based on a certain view of Matthew 25:46: "Then they will go away to eternal punishment, but the righteous to eternal life." This argument stems from Augustine and is used by almost every traditionalist.[57] Put simply, it states that since eternal life is forever, punishment must also last forever. Many traditionalists would base their entire commitment to endless torment on this one verse alone. The obvious parallelism between eternal life and eternal punishment is what makes this argument seem to stick. Since the punishment of the lost must last as long as the life of the righteous, how can conditionalists argue for only a temporary punishment in hell? Are they willing to admit, given the parallelism, that eternal life is also temporary? Since conditionalists do not deny that eternal life is forever, then they must be guilty of using the word *eternal* in two different senses.[58]

---

[57] Alan W. Gomes, "Evangelicals and the Annihilation of Hell", *Christian Research Journal* Spring (1991): 18.

[58] See Erickson 231. Traditionalists assume that conditionalists are arguing this way because of their own assumption that eternal punishment requires eternal consciousness. Conditionalists, however, reject this assumption. Conditionalists believe that the result of punishment is eternal, not the process. They do *not* use the word eternal in two different senses; they believe that life requires eternal consciousness but punishment does not. Millard Erickson is a good example of a traditionalist who ignores a perfectly logical account of the parallelism in Matthew 25:46. After noting that Edward Fudge explains eternal punishment as eternal in result, he accuses him of not dealing with the

This argument only works if we smuggle the word *conscious* into the meaning of the word *punishment*.[59] Traditionalists simply assume that because eternal life involves consciousness, then punishment must also. What they overlook, however, is that the contrast between eternal life and punishment is presented in other parts of the New Testament as a contrast between eternal life and death (Rom. 6:23). Life certainly involves consciousness, but death does not, except when speaking of the living who are "dead in transgressions and sins."[60] Conditionalists do not, in fact, believe that life is eternal and punishment is temporary; they believe that both are eternal. What is really at issue in this argument is the nature of punishment.

Traditionalists assume that punishment requires consciousness. Alan Gomes writes, "Punishment demands the existence of the one being punished."[61] W.G.T. Shedd writes, "The extinction of consciousness is not of the nature of punishment."[62] These dogmatic pronouncements are

---

parallelism. How has Fudge failed to deal with the parallelism, except that he refuses to accept Erickson's unnecessary assumption? After all, Matthew 25:46 does not say that punishment requires eternal consciousness. Erickson, like most traditionalists, simply does not see that it is the nature of punishment—not the word *eternal*—that is at issue in this key passage. By focusing on the word *eternal*, he is helping to perpetuate the confusion surrounding this controversial passage.

[59] Clark H. Pinnock, "The Destruction of the Finally Impenitent", *Criswell Theological Review* 4 (1990): 256.

[60] Certainly our understanding of physical death includes the idea of unconsciousness. Traditionalists consider the death of the body as virtually irrelevant to the concept of eternal death, despite the fact that we think of death mainly in this way.

[61] Gomes 18.

[62] Shedd 92.

another example of how traditionalists import concepts into the Bible without proving them from the Bible. Punishments generally involve the conscious experience of the one punished, but there are also punishments of deprivation. The death penalty in the Bible is the prime example of a punishment that deprives the offender of earthly life. The act of putting the offender to death is only part of the punishment. The main part of the punishment is depriving the offender of the experience of life he would have had if he had not been punished in this way. In essence, the penalty involves the loss of consciousness—the consciousness of earthly life.[63]

Another way to describe the mistake of traditionalists is that they confuse punishment with punishing. An eternal punishment is not necessarily an eternal punishing. Punishments can have eternal results without an ongoing process.[64] In terms of final punishment, this means that the fires of hell will not torment forever, but the final destruction caused by those fires will have an everlasting effect. The sinner's punishment, then, is eternal destruction. This in no way compromises Matthew 25:46. It is perfectly

---

[63] Surprisingly, Shedd makes this very point about the death penalty but fails to see that his own admission contradicts his assumption that a punishment must be consciously experienced in order to be a punishment: "The human penalty that approaches nearest to the Divine, is capital punishment. There is more of the purely retributive element in this than in any other. The reformatory element is wanting. And this punishment has a kind of endlessness. Death is a finality. It forever separates the murderer from earthly society, even as future punishment separates forever from the society of God and heaven." (131) Given these words, how could Shedd have failed to see that consciousness is *not* of the nature of punishment in every case?

[64] The next chapter will elaborate this point in more detail.

consistent, providing the assumptions of eternal consciousness and eternal punishing are not read into the passage.

The problem with Matthew 25:46 is that it does not stand on its own. The nature of punishment must be determined from the rest of the Bible, and the Bible does not teach that punishments demand the existence of the one being punished in every case. The death penalty requires that the offender be alive only long enough to receive the punishment; after that, the death of the offender becomes the very point of the punishment. The death penalty is a good example of a punishment focused on a result rather than a process.

The favorite arguments for endless torment do not prove the traditional position. Their wide acceptance is based on an uncritical acceptance of certain assumptions that are smuggled into the arguments to make them sound. These assumptions are easily exposed by many counterexamples taken from the Bible itself. It is time to break the habit of looking at the Bible through the twin lenses of infinite guilt and eternal punishing. Once these glasses are removed, the biblical doctrine of God's justice and mercy becomes clear and acceptable.

Chapter 3
ETERNAL THINGS THAT DON'T LAST FOREVER

What ideas does the word *eternal* bring to mind? Most think of the word *eternal* as a synonym for *forever*, *never ending*, or *everlasting*. The concept of eternal as forever is so common in the everyday use of our language that most do not consider that many things called eternal in the Bible do not actually last forever. Any careful reader of the Bible would notice this, but most do not because of our habitual association of eternal things with things that last forever.

The word *eternal* (*aionios*) is an adjective and in both testaments literally means "age-long". The noun form of the word (*aion*) is translated *age* in Matthew 24:3 and other places. The Old Testament equivalent (*olam*) has roughly the same meaning. The Bible really does not have a word that matches our abstract concept of eternity. For Westerners, anything eternal lasts forever and is timeless.[65]

---
[65] This idea was developed in Greek philosophy and by Plato in particular.

The Bible uses the adjective *eternal* more flexibly. There are many things in the Bible that are referred to as eternal that do not last forever. There are also cases where the word is used to emphasize the divine quality of something (Jude 7; John 17:3). There are cases where the usage of the word approximates our common use, but these refer to God himself. God is called "the Eternal God" in three places in the Bible (Gen. 21:3; Deut. 33:27; Rom. 16:26).[66] Only God may be spoken of as timeless. Time is created by God (Heb. 1:2), and even the redeemed will exist forever *in time*.[67] Therefore, our abstract Western concept of eternity does not apply to the Bible straight across the board.

The words *lasting* and *perpetual* are often better words to describe the biblical use of the word *eternal*. Something that is perpetual lasts as long as it is intended to by God. By looking at examples in both Testaments, it will become clear that eternal things do not necessarily last forever. This, in turn, has a profound affect on how we understand final judgment.

---

[66] These statistics are based on the New International Version of the Bible.

[67] Hebrews 1:2 is the key passage in the Bible showing that time is created: "but in these last days he has spoken to us by his Son, whom he appointed heir of all things, and through whom he made the universe." In the original language, the phrase, "through whom he made the universe," is literally *through whom he made the ages*. The Greek does intend to convey the idea of the creation of all things, but it does so in terms of the temporal framework of the creation. In other words, God created both the things of the universe and the time of their existence. In modern terms, we would say that God created the universe in all its dimensions, including matter, space, and time. Many Bible readers have been misled by the KJV rendering of Revelation 10:6, which says "that there shall be time no longer." This verse is not saying that time will end; it is saying that "there will be no more delay." According to the next verse, "the mystery of God" was to be accomplished without further delay.

Eternal Things in the Old Testament

Genesis 17:8 illustrates the principle that something eternal lasts only as long as it is supposed to last:

> 8 The whole land of Canaan, where you are now an alien, I will give as an everlasting possession to you and your descendants after you; and I will be their God.

Canaan is spoken of here as an everlasting possession (literally, an eternal possession), despite the fact that it was intended to typify heaven. Its central city, Jerusalem, was typical of the Heavenly Jerusalem, which is the true home of God's people. As a type of the heavenly city, Jerusalem's location on a hill, its Temple, priests, and office of kingship were all meant to picture the redemptive realities of the New Covenant. In Galatians 4:26, Paul says, "the Jerusalem that is above is free, and she is our mother." By contrast, the earthly Jerusalem of Paul's day represented the spiritual slavery of those who sought righteousness before God on the basis of meritorious law-works (4:25). The writer of Hebrews spoke of the people of God as those who "have [already] come to Mount Zion, to the heavenly Jerusalem, the city of the living God." Obviously, Canaan was not meant to be an eternal possession as most people think of eternity.

Genesis 49:26 speaks of the mountains as eternal: "Your father's blessings are greater than the blessings of the ancient mountains, than the bounty of the age-old hills." The "age-old hills" are literally the *eternal hills*. The Hebrew word *olam* is used to point to the lasting or enduring quality of the mountains, not to the idea that they exist into eternity.

Exodus 12:14, 17 speaks of the Passover as a perpetual or *eternal* ordinance: "This is a day you are to commemorate; for the generations to come you shall celebrate it as a festival to the LORD—a lasting ordinance." The common teaching of the Christian Church throughout history has been that the Passover is definitely not eternal in the sense of never-ending. The Lord's Supper is actually the fulfillment of the Passover because Christ is "our Passover", and the Lord's Supper commemorates the slaying of Christ, the Passover Lamb (1 Cor. 5:7). The Jewish Passover was part of the Old Covenant system, a system which by the time the book of Hebrews was written was "obsolete and aging" and soon to disappear (Heb. 8:13).

An unusual use of the word *eternal* in the Old Testament is found in Jonah 2:5-6. Speaking of his incarceration in the belly of the great fish, Jonah speaks of his experience over three days:

> 5 The engulfing waters threatened me, the deep surrounded me; seaweed was wrapped around my head.
> 6 To the roots of the mountains I sank down; the earth beneath **barred me in forever**. But you brought my life up from the pit, O LORD my God.

This passage is striking because it demonstrates a characteristic of *forever* that is generally overlooked in the Bible. Jonah uses the word hyperbolically. He was only in

CHAPTER 3 ▪ Eternal Things That Don't Last Forever

the belly of the fish for three days, but he describes it as an eternity. This is much the same way we use the word when we say "the waiter took forever." This usage occurs elsewhere in the Bible and proves that God can describe certain temporary things using the language of forever.

Many traditionalists argue that things pertaining to this age may be referred to as eternal when they are actually temporary, but things referring to the age to come are always endless. Based on Jesus' distinction between this age and the age to come (Mt. 12:32), traditionalists believe that "the present age, or *aeon*, is 'time;' the future age, or *aeon*, is 'eternity.'"[68] This distinction between "time" and "eternity" is employed to argue that one need only determine which age is being referred to in the Bible in order to determine whether the eternal thing pertaining to that age is temporary or everlasting.[69] Traditionalists attempt to use this distinction between time and eternity to justify endless torment by saying that if punishment takes place in the age to come, then it must last forever because eternity is forever. Conditionalists could easily agree with this logic, while simply denying the assumption

---

[68] Shedd 80.

[69] The Bible does not make a strict philosophical distinction between time and eternity, since even eternity will involve the continuation of time. In fact, the present age is referred to a series of ages (1 Cor. 2:7; Eph. 3:9; Col. 1:26), and so is the age to come (Rom. 1:25; Gal. 1:5; 1 Tim. 1:17). In Colossians 1:5, the age to come is referred to as *the ages of the ages* in the original language. In the New Testament, the ages of history are separated from the ages of eternity by the consummation (Rev. 20:7-15). The biblical distinction, then, is not between time and a timeless eternity. That conception is a Greek philosophical idea.

of eternal punishing. Conditionalists also believe that the punishment of the age to come is endless; they simply do not believe that the punishment requires eternal consciousness. Unfortunately, traditionalists do not often do their conditionalist opponents the courtesy of acknowledging the precise point of disagreement between them.[70] The disagreement is not about the distinction between history and eternity; it is about the eternity of the self and the nature of punishment.

Eternal Things in the New Testament

When it comes to eternal things in the New Testament, it is important to notice some of the different words that are used in connection with the adjective *eternal*. The word *eternal* is often used with nouns of action. For example, we read about eternal judgment, eternal salvation, eternal destruction, and eternal fire. What is interesting in these uses is that they focus on a result rather than a process. In other words, it is not that the action itself continues forever, but rather the result of the action lasts forever. Only a few examples are needed to make this clear. The writer of Hebrews speaks of both judgment and salvation as eternal:

> 8 Although he was a son, he learned obedience from what he suffered 9 and, once made perfect, he became

---

[70] In fairness to traditionalists, it is acknowledged that conditionalists are sometimes fuzzy on the genuine points of difference as well. In an area like this that has not had the benefit of open and fruitful dialogue, there is bound to be a great deal of miscommunication, because the precise points at issue are not clear to either side in the debate.

> the source of **eternal salvation** for all who obey him. (Heb. 5:8-9)

> 1 Therefore let us leave the elementary teachings about Christ and go on to maturity, not laying again the foundation of repentance from acts that lead to death, and of faith in God, 2 instruction about baptisms, the laying on of hands, the resurrection of the dead, and *eternal judgment*. (Heb. 6:1-2).

The writer of Hebrews does not intend to teach that Christ became the source of an eternal process of saving. According to the Bible, the process of saving is consummated on the Day of Judgment when the elect are declared righteous in Christ. The result of the saving process is eternal salvation, a condition produced by the saving work of Christ. Eternal judgment should also be understood in the same way. James Nichols summarizes the use of *eternal* with nouns of action:

> Accordingly, "eternal judgment" (Heb. 6:2) is not endless judging. No one supposes that the judgment will last forever, but its results will. "Eternal salvation" (Heb. 5:9) certainly does not mean endless saving, but that the results of the salvation wrought by Christ will be endless. "Eternal sin" (Mark 3:29) is not the same as endless sinning; it is a sin which has an endless result—no forgiveness now or later.[71]

---

[71] Nichols 132.

These examples illuminate the previous discussion of eternal punishment. Eternal punishment does not mean eternal punishing. It is remarkable that traditionalists do not even consider the above examples when reading Matthew 25:46. The tendency to ignore eternal results in favor of an eternal process of punishment is simply based on a habit of belief and the lack of self-criticism and fresh ideas within traditional circles. The danger in such habits of belief is that errors seem obvious and self-evident only because another point of view is never presented to challenge the status quo interpretation. Could this be the reason why challenges to endless torment are often met with a smug indifference?

A favorite "proof text" of traditionalists is found in 2 Thessalonians 1:9, which describes Christ's punishment of the persecutors of God's people:

> 9 They will be punished with everlasting destruction and shut out from the presence of the Lord and from the majesty of his power....

Based on what has been said, it would seem quite natural to take Paul's words to refer to the termination of God's enemies by the "blazing fire" of his coming. Everlasting destruction refers to irrevocable destruction without the prospect of forgiveness or restoration to life. Traditionalists, however, can see only an endless process of destroying that requires eternal consciousness. Many will point to the second part of this verse as evidence of eternal consciousness. Since the lost are to be "shut out from the presence of the Lord," does not this imply their continued existence? As a matter fact, there is no reason why it should. All who are destroyed in Gehenna will certainly be shut out from the Lord's presence.[72] Again, there is a predisposition to smuggle the idea of conscious existence into every verse that speaks of final judgment. It is not that the passages really suggest eternal consciousness; traditionalists are simply in the habit of bringing the idea to every passage they encounter where the word *eternal* is found. What Paul is saying is that the enemies of God will be destroyed, never to return from the oblivion of eternal punishment.

Eternal Torment in the Book of Revelation

There are many Christians who would listen to the argument for conditional immortality if it were not for two verses in the book of Revelation. Many would agree that the biblical data can easily be harmonized with the idea of endless destruction, except for two seemingly unequivocal verses in the last book of the Bible: Revelation 14:11 and 20:10. These two verses are relied upon so heavily by many traditionalists that they have no trouble sweeping aside the import of the destruction language of the Bible for the sake

[72] This tendency to assume eternal consciousness is peculiar in light of the fact that we often speak of those long dead as if they still existed as persons. Traditionalists might argue that the reason we do this is because we know that our relatives still exist as persons somewhere. However, this does not explain the speech of those who do not believe in an afterlife. They often speak of relatives and even pets as those who are no longer with us. This is because persons continue to exist in our memory. They have a kind of existence that justifies speaking of them in the way Paul does in 2 Thessalonians 1:9.

of these two verses alone.[73]

Given the importance of these two verses in the argument for endless torment, we must pay careful attention to their interpretation:

> 9 A third angel followed them and said in a loud voice: "If anyone worships the beast and his image and receives his mark on the forehead or on the hand, 10 he, too, will drink of the wine of God's fury, which has been poured full strength into the cup of his wrath. He will be tormented with burning sulfur in the presence of the holy angels and of the Lamb. 11 And the smoke of their torment rises for ever and ever. There is no rest day or night for those who worship the beast and his image, or for anyone who receives the mark of his name." (Rev. 14:9-11)

> 10 And the devil, who deceived them, was thrown into the lake of burning sulfur, where the beast and the false prophet had been thrown. They will be tormented day and night for ever and ever. (Rev. 20:10)

Revelation 14:11 and 20:10 certainly can be taken to teach the doctrine of endless torment if we restrict ourselves to a surface view of the language. One of the great problems with traditionalists is that they often bring to the biblical text preconceived notions about the nature of biblical

---

[73] Peterson 169. Peterson references these two verses again and again in his book. Whenever he comes to a verse that can be understood in a conditionalist sense, he simply quotes these two verses to prove that a conditionalist interpretation of any passage is simply impossible. Unfortunately, he never questions what he takes to be the obvious meaning of these verses. If he were to look at the Old Testament for the antecedents of the language of Revelation, he might not be as confident of the "plain meaning" of these verses.

language and how literally it should be understood. Modern Western readers often forget that their own view of language is heavily influenced by our modern preoccupation with precision and linguistic accuracy. The biblical writers, however, thought and wrote out of an oriental rather than an occidental world view, which is why the Bible is not written like a newspaper or a scientific journal. The Bible makes use of some literary styles that are frankly odd to the modern Western mind. The apocalyptic genre of the book of Revelation is one such literary style that is generally misunderstood by Christians. In the interest of maintaining a commitment to the literal interpretation of the Bible, many Evangelicals especially have distorted the interpretation of the book of Revelation to unreasonable proportions.[74] Before settling on a surface view of Revelation 14:11 and 20:10, it is important to look first at

[74] John F. Walvoord, rev. of *The Fire That Consumes*, by Edward William Fudge, *Bibliotheca Sacra* Oct. - Dec. 1984: 364. Walvoord writes off anyone as a liberal who violates his Dispensational standard of literal interpretation. Interpreters like Walvoord have failed to recognize that literary genre define the limits of interpretation, not a preconceived standard of literalness. He believes that any use of nonliteral interpretation leaves the interpreter free to make whatever he wants out of the Bible: "If the interpreter is free to take in a nonliteral sense any statement that teaches something contrary to his doctrine, it is obvious that it is not difficult to go through Scripture and establish a point of view which the Scriptures actually do not teach." This statement is inconsistent because it ignores the fact that Walvoord himself resorts to nonliteral interpretations of passages where he believes the literary genre requires it. Each literary genre of the Bible has its own recognized characteristics that define how that literature is to be properly interpreted. Only a dishonest interpreter who violates those characteristics can make whatever he wants out of the Bible. Walvoord's warnings against nonliteral interpretation are another example of the scare tactics used by many Evangelicals to keep their followers from straying from some of their own flawed hyperorthodox views. By presenting deviations from their own principles as compromises with liberalism, they frighten their followers into obscurantism.

where this language comes from. Since over ninety percent of the book of Revelation is made up of Old Testament quotations and allusions, we would expect to find the source of the language in the Old Testament. Revelation 14:11 and 20:10 are both allusions to Isaiah 34:8-10:

> 8 For the LORD has a day of vengeance, a year of retribution, to uphold Zion's cause. 9 Edom's streams will be turned into pitch, her dust into burning sulfur; her land will become blazing pitch! 10 It will not be quenched night and day; its smoke will rise forever. From generation to generation it will lie desolate; no one will ever pass through it again.

This prophecy refers to the destruction of the Edomites by the Babylonians in Old Testament times. Interestingly, even though this prophecy is already fulfilled, Isaiah speaks of Edom's streams and land as being on fire—"her land will become blazing pitch!" The prophet goes on to say that this fire will not be quenched night and day and that its smoke will rise forever. Here is another unquenchable fire with eternally rising smoke. What should strike traditionalists— but for some reason does not—is that the land of Edom was never literally on fire, nor is it still burning. We know where the land of Edom is located, so it is relatively easy to verify this. Here we find the language of eternal fire and smoke where there is none. Why would Isaiah speak of God's judgment on Edom in these terms if they were not meant literally?

CHAPTER 3 • Eternal Things That Don't Last Forever

The answer is to be found in the apocalyptic literary genre and the oriental mentality of the Jewish people. The expression in Isaiah is another example of hyperbole. Isaiah is describing the complete and utter destruction of the Edomites in emotionally charged words. Hyperbole is intentional overstatement for emotional effect, and from a literal point of view, the prophet certainly overstated Edom's destruction by the Babylonians. In fact, to take Isaiah's words literally, we would have to charge him with falsehood.[75] Hyperbole, however, is a main characteristic of apocalyptic language in the Bible, so there is no reason to charge the biblical writer with teaching falsehood. Apocalyptic language is not meant to be taken literally; in fact, to do so in a case like this is to misinterpret the Bible.

The apostle John alludes to this passage of Isaiah in both 14:11 and 20:10. Both John and Isaiah refer to smoke that rises forever; both also refer to fire that burns day and night. The question that remains for traditionalists to answer is simple: If Isaiah was not describing an everlasting burning and torment for the inhabitants of Edom, why

---

[75] Evangelicals can undermine biblical authority by insisting on strictly literal interpretation. Any intelligent person can see that many things in the Bible, if taken in a strictly literal sense, are falsehoods. In essence, some Evangelical interpreters may be setting people up to reject the Bible. It does not take long for an intelligent person committed to the idea of strict literalism to become frustrated with the Bible's lack of scientific precision. If we interpret the Bible from a proper literary approach, we do not encounter as many problems. The Bible can easily be shown to be internally consistent with itself. One of the great lessons of Church history is that liberalism is a reaction to hyperorthodox rationalism. Therefore, those who piously cry "literal interpretation" must beware of acting as pied pipers leading some of their followers over the cliff into liberalism.

should that same type of language be taken differently in the New Testament passages that allude to it, especially when other biblical passages seem clearly to teach the final termination of the lost? Unfortunately, traditionalists rarely, if ever, even notice that the hyperbolic judgment language of the Old Testament calls into question their interpretation of the Revelation passages. They simply take their view as the obvious one without ever looking at the Old Testament. Isaiah 34:8-10 is only one of many passages where hyperbole is used in the Old Testament. Several other passages testify to the naive approach traditionalists take to the judgment language of the Bible.[76] When Isaiah speaks of everlasting burning and smoke, he is referring to the complete and utter destruction of the inhabitants of Edom. Similarly, when John uses the same kind of apocalyptic language, there is no reason to believe that he is teaching anything different than Isaiah taught using the same kind of language.

There are a few Evangelicals who recognize that Isaiah 34:10 is talking about a temporary judgment as if it were endless. In the interest of maintaining their commitment to endless torment, they come up with a rather clever but implausible explanation of the language. They will say that Isaiah is speaking prophetically, describing a temporal judgment in terms of the eternal judgment to come. In other words, the eternal judgment of hell fire intrudes into history in Isaiah's description of Edom's punishment. This

---

[76] See also Is.13; 24; 34:1-10; Ez. 32:1-12; Mic. 1:3-4; Nah. 1:3-6; 2 Pet. 3:10.

CHAPTER 3 • Eternal Things That Don't Last Forever

approach, which is aptly called *intrusionism*, is meant to explain how a temporary judgment can be described as if it were an eternal judgment. In fact, it simply assumes what needs to be proved. Instead of looking at the way the Old Testament writers use this language, traditionalists are determined to find some way to read endless torment into these passages so that they cannot be used against the position.

The problems with this approach should be obvious. First, Isaiah says that *the land* of Edom is on fire and burns forever. Nothing in the teaching of final punishment speaks of land burning in the fire of hell; only people experience eternal torment according to the traditional view. Second, Isaiah clearly says that the actual land of Edom is subject to fire and desolation throughout the generations to come. Interestingly, after describing the land as being on fire forever, he goes on to speak of the land as a desolate place inhabited by desert creatures (vs. 11-15). Surely Isaiah knew that his readers could figure out that he did not mean to literally teach that the land was to be on fire, for how could desert creatures inhabit land that was on fire? If Isaiah knew this, then why did he speak in such a confusing way? The answer is that the Jews understood this mode of communication and were not confused by it. They understood the emotive power of such overstatements in communicating God's wrath and his intent to destroy his enemies. The problem is with modern people who do not understand this kind of language; some will not be happy with the Bible until they can reduce everything in it to a literal proposition.

Some Christians feel unnerved by the prospect of accepting hyperbolic language in the Bible. After all, it seems so imprecise and misleading on God's part to use such language just for emotional effect. When people exaggerate, we usually consider them at least somewhat dishonest. Therefore, how can we believe that God would resort to such overstatement in speaking of his judgment on Edom? Is not a description of a temporal judgment as an endless judgment something like using an atomic flyswatter? The fact that people have such attitudes toward apocalyptic language in the Bible shows one thing clearly: Some do have preconceptions about how God can and cannot express himself through the writers of the Bible. It would seem more fitting in those who believe that the Bible is the Word of God to simply allow God to say what he wants in the way he wants. If hyperbolic expressions were not considered unethical or imprecise by the Jews, why should we have problems with them? The Bible can use any literary genre to communicate truth, including myth.[77]

---

[77] The Bible does, in fact, use myth to communicate truth. Job 26 and Psalm 89 refer to Rahab, the water monster. God slays Rahab, showing his supremacy over the waters and the entire creation. In this case, the Bible is using a pagan myth for apologetic purposes. The parables of Jesus would also be completely ethical even if they were mere stories and not based on fact. How many preachers tell stories from their church pulpits not knowing if all the details are precisely true? These stories are aptly called "sermon illustrations." Most people would not accuse a minister of lying if he used a sermon illustration that was somewhat stylized for the sake of his sermon.

CHAPTER 3 ▪ Eternal Things That Don't Last Forever

For most traditionalists, the biggest hurdle in taking Revelation 14:11 and 20:10 as hyperbolic is simply breaking the habit of taking them literally. If we compare Scripture with Scripture, it is more natural to take these verses as hyperbolic expressions of the complete destruction of the lost. It does not, however, *seem* natural to someone who has believed differently for a long time. The psychological barrier to seeing a better interpretation of the Bible is seldom recognized by traditionalists. When they read an argument, even a good one, they often base their assent on how they *feel* about the argument, instead of adjusting their feelings to the merits of the argument.

By recognizing the characteristics of biblical apocalyptic, other passages come to light in new and meaningful ways. As an example, consider Revelation 20:12-14, which speaks of the final judgment:

> 12 And I saw the dead, great and small, standing before the throne, and books were opened. Another book was opened, which is the book of life. The dead were judged according to what they had done as recorded in the books. 13 The sea gave up the dead that were in it, and death and Hades gave up the dead that were in them, and each person was judged according to what he had done. 14 Then death and Hades were thrown into the lake of fire. The lake of fire is the second death.

In verse 14, John says that death and Hades were thrown into the lake of fire. On the traditional view, we would expect death and the grave to be tormented forever, just like all the other inhabitants of hell. Given that death and Hades are not actual persons, such an interpretation seems rather strange. It seems clear, however, that God intends to destroy death and the grave, removing them from the universe forever. And this agrees with what Paul says in 1 Corinthians 15:24-26:

> 24 Then the end will come, when he hands over the kingdom to God the Father after he has destroyed all dominion, authority and power. 25 For he must reign until he has put all his enemies under his feet. 26 The last enemy to be destroyed is death.

The destruction of death, according to Paul, seems clearly to mean the end of death. What else could it mean, since death does not exist as a person who could be tormented forever? The destruction or end of death and the grave in Revelation 20:14 confirms that John's language is perfectly compatible with the idea of complete and utter destruction rather than endless torment. Even though it may seem natural to take Revelation 20:10 as a literal description of the endless torment of the devil, the beast, and the false prophet, we must remember that the language of Scripture, not what seems natural to us, is to govern the way we understand John's words. Traditionalists like to point out that John uses the strongest expression possible to describe endless torment ("forever and ever").[78] But they fail to point out that this language would also be appropriate

---

[78] Gomes 18.

CHAPTER 3 • Eternal Things That Don't Last Forever

in a hyperbolic expression of complete destruction.[79] They fail to point it out because they do not even consider the use of hyperbole in the Bible's judgment language. This is the single greatest oversight of the traditional position, so great, in fact, that it is not even mentioned in any traditional treatment of the duration of hell.[80]

Surprisingly, there is one traditionalist author who recognizes that the New Testament writers do use "rabbinic hyperbole" in connection with the doctrine of hell. He does not, however, apply what he sees to the duration of hell. After recognizing "rabbinic hyperbole or colorful speech" in the words of Jesus, he goes on to say:

> The same is true with the images of hell we find in the New Testament. Their purpose is not to give the reader a literal picture of torment, but a symbolic one. In Jewish

---

[79] Jude 13 should also be understood as hyperbolic: "They are wild waves of the sea, foaming up their shame; wandering stars, for whom blackest darkness has been reserved forever." On the surface, this verse could also be understood to teach endless torment. But given the consumption/destruction language of the Bible and the nature of biblical apocalyptic, a surface reading of the passage is not the best approach. The conditionalist view of Jude 13 and passages like it actually makes the Bible more internally consistent. The traditional view really sacrifices the coherence of the Bible to some degree in the interest of literalistic interpretations. Faced with a choice between a more internally consistent Bible and a more reasonable view of hell on the one hand, and a less consistent Bible and eternal torment on the other, most people would wisely adopt conditionalism.

[80] It is possible that someone has mentioned this point somewhere, but it is certainly not mentioned in the current authoritative literature written by traditionalists. It is difficult to avoid the conclusion that the idea of hyperbole in the judgment language of Scripture simply has not occurred to traditionalists. This is probably the reason why they represent their own view of the language as obvious and plain to all. If you are aware of only one approach to a problem, that approach is likely to seem like the obvious one.

and Greek literature we often find vivid pictures of hell, but generally they did not intend their fiery descriptions to be taken literally. When Gentile converts to Christianity encountered hellfire descriptions similar to those they had grown up with, they would naturally interpret those portraits as symbols representing the wrath of God. If they were mistaken and hell was indeed a place of literal heat and smoke, one would expect to find a correction of this view somewhere in the literature of the Bible. But, of course, there is none.[81]

While this is a remarkable confirmation from a traditionalist that the language about hell is hyperbolic, it is equally remarkable that it never occurs to him to apply this insight to the duration of hell. Based on Isaiah 34 and other passages noted above, the hyperbolic language of fire and smoke applies just as much to the duration of hell as it does to what hell will actually be like. Why, then, does it never occur to this traditionalist to see what Isaiah saw so clearly? It is because traditionalists have no intention of letting symbolic descriptions of hell threaten the idea that hell is forever. Once it is admitted, however, that the language about hell is hyperbolic, there is no escaping the implications of passages like Isaiah 34. The language of the biblical writers does apply to the duration of hell, and traditionalists like Crockett are arbitrarily limiting the application of this vital insight to only one aspect of the doctrine of hell.

---

[81] Crockett 52.

Another passage that is often used to counter the idea of the final destruction of the impenitent is Revelation 22:15. This verse is contrasting the inhabitants of the New Jerusalem with those who are cast out:

> 15 Outside are the dogs, those who practice magic arts, the sexually immoral, the murderers, the idolaters and everyone who loves and practices falsehood.

Traditionalists will argue that this verse proves that the lost must exist forever because they are spoken of as being *outside* the heavenly Jerusalem.[82] Conditionalists do not deny that the lost are excluded from the city or that they exist for a time outside the city. They simply do not say that the "dogs" exist *forever* outside the city before they are destroyed, and neither does John. This verse is completely compatible with the conditionalist belief that the wicked will suffer as persons "outside the city" before their final destruction. Conditionalists do not bring the assumption to the verse that just because some will exist outside the city, they must, therefore, exist forever.

There are many things in the Bible that are called eternal, but they do not all last forever. In looking at the way the biblical writers think of time, it should not be surprising that Westerners have misunderstood the way the Bible uses the words for time and eternity. The traditional view of eternal torment represents a simplistic approach to the biblical literature. For many, Matthew 25:46 and

---

[82] Peterson 96n, Crockett 76.

Revelation 14:11 and 20:10 are all they need to persuade them that the destruction language of the Bible cannot refer to the termination of those outside of Christ. These verses, however, are not as simple as the traditionalist would like to think they are, because the Bible is not a Western book. As an Eastern book, it is richer, more subtle, and more colorful. If we acknowledge this and learn to enjoy the peculiarities of the biblical revelation, we will realize that the Bible becomes more profound and liberating than it was before. Perhaps the greatest liberation of all comes when we realize that the doctrine of endless conscious torment is not taught in the Bible at all but is, in fact, a misinterpretation by well-meaning Christians.

Conclusion
IS CONDITIONAL IMMORTALITY A HERESY?

A Call for Balanced Judgment

> 9 And this is my prayer: that your love may abound more and more in knowledge and depth of insight, 10 so that you may be able to discern what is best and may be pure and blameless until the day of Christ, 11 filled with the fruit of righteousness that comes through Jesus Christ—to the glory and praise of God. (Phil. 1:9-11)

The Bible contains many great prayers, but this prayer of Paul for the Philippians is, in my opinion, one of the greatest. Especially significant is his desire that his readers "may be able to discern what is best." By increasing knowledge and insight, their ability to distinguish between the better and the best would also improve. The need for balanced judgment and discernment is especially relevant to the controversy surrounding hell. While the biblical language about hell is not ambiguous, it is also not simplistic. Traditionalists have claimed that the plain and simple teaching of the Bible is that those outside of Christ are to be tormented forever in the lake of fire. They have done so, however, in the face of the very bold imagery of consumption and destruction—imagery that certainly calls into question their belief in endless torment.

Instead of considering other interpretive possibilities, traditionalists have been unwilling to consider conditional immortality, even branding those who embrace it as liberals, cultists, and heretics. They charge their opponents with sentimentalism and scripture-twisting, despite the fact that conditionalism does a better job harmonizing the biblical witness than they have done themselves.[83] At the very least, traditionalists should be willing to acknowledge that conditional immortality represents a serious attempt to do justice to a difficult biblical issue without compromising the integrity of the Bible. Unfortunately, advocates of endless torment have failed to evaluate conditionalism fairly or to appreciate a serious biblical attempt to relieve the emotional pressure that the doctrine of endless torment creates in believers and unbelievers alike.

---

[83] The charge of heresy really makes no sense at all given the straightforward handling of the Bible by conditionalists. This approach is summarized as follows: "Evangelical Conditionalists maintain that the primary, literal and obvious meaning of biblical terms (e.g., life, death, destruction, perish, mortal, immortal, and *Gehenna*) is that unbelievers will cease to exist after judgment and that only those who trust in Christ will receive immortality." David A. Dean, "Is Conditionalism an Evangelical Heresy?" *Resurrection* 92.3 (1989) 10.

CONCLUSION • Is Conditional Immortality A Heresy?

This closed-minded attitude on the part of many traditionalists is curious, because they are often quite understanding when it comes to other areas of controversy. Many are more than willing to accept the validity of different eschatological options because of the difficulty of the subject matter. Premillennialism, Postmillennialism, Amillennialism, and Preterism are all represented among Christians, and many denominations do not take an official position on the subject of future eschatology. Rarely do those with a definite conviction in this area go around branding those who differ with them heretics. The eternal torment of the lost, however, is another story. Even when a strong case is put forth by devout scholars such as Stott, Fudge, and Hughes, traditionalists are still unwilling to acknowledge that there may be, in fact, good reasons why other Christians disagree with them.[84] John Stott is absolutely correct in pointing out that it is high time that conditional immortality be accepted as a legitimate Evangelical position.[85] The continued resistance to this suggestion by traditionalists reflects a lack of discernment and a need for greater knowledge and insight into the biblical passages that speak to the issue of final punishment.

---

[84] The fine work of Clark Pinnock in this area is also worthy of recognition. Pinnock is not as highly respected among many Evangelicals because of positions he has taken on the sovereignty of God and the inspiration of the Bible. Despite the controversy generated by his writings, there is no doubt that Pinnock is one of the finest theological writers Evangelicalism has produced. His writing is powerful, provocative, and informative, and his published defenses of conditional immortality are among his most worthwhile offerings.

[85] Edwards and Stott 320.

Many of the reasons for this resistance have been covered already, but there are others that also deserve attention. There are several myths that surround conditional immortality, and these are perpetuated by traditionalists in order to maintain their perceived monopoly on the truth about hell. Like the doctrine of the immortality of the soul, these myths must be exposed so that the arguments for conditional immortality may appear before traditionalists unclouded by the fog of the myth-makers.

A Call for Clear Vision

Perhaps the greatest myth that keeps traditionalists from looking at hell from a different perspective is the falsehood that conditional immortality represents a denial of hell. For some reason, traditionalists like to present the view as though committing to it is the same as saying that there is no hell at all. Aside from being an outright distortion of the conditionalist position, it is an obvious attempt to prejudice one's audience. Consider, for example, the title of a well-known article by Alan Gomes, which attempts to refute conditional immortality: "Evangelicals and the Annihilation of Hell." Does conditional immortality represent the annihilation of hell, or does it represent a rejection of endless torment in the fires of hell? Conditionalists speak of the ultimate annihilation of the enemies of God, but this is the result of the painful and destructive force of hell itself. Gomes plays a rhetorical trick on his readers by making them think of conditional

CONCLUSION • Is Conditional Immortality A Heresy?

immortality as a denial of hell when it is no such thing. Such an unscholarly tactic is unworthy of those who claim to believe in the ninth commandment.

Also related to this myth is the one that attempts to persuade people that the ultimate destruction of the lost amounts to letting people off easy. This myth is based on the mistaken notion that there is no penal suffering in hell to repay the sinner for all the wrong done in this life. Most conditionalists are not simple annihilationists like the Jehovah's Witnesses. Traditionalists know this, but they do not make the distinction in their writings, so their readers are left with the impression that anyone who denies the traditional view is letting people off too easy.[86] In fact, conditionalists do not let people off too easy. Jesus describes hell as "weeping and gnashing of teeth." Just because conditionalists do not consign people to the blast furnace of hell forever, are they thereby guilty of letting people off too easy? The sufferings of hell will be justly proportional to the sins committed in this life (Luke 12:47-48). Does God have to inflict endless torment just to prove that he is not letting people off easy? To listen to the arguments of traditionalists, it would seem so. Ironically, traditionalists

---

[86] A typical example of this is found in Blanchard: "For the annihilationist, there is no possibility of perfect justice or the righting of wrongs. Good will remain unrewarded and evil unpunished. The serial murderer and the tiny child, the rapist and the kindly old lady, the ruthless dictator and the gentle nurse, everything they are and everything they have been and done will be wiped out of existence." (67) Blanchard should say who these conditionalists are who believe that good will remain unrewarded and evil unpunished, because there is not one conditionalist who believes this. This is an example of the "straw man" fallacy. Such arguments are common in traditionalist literature.

who spank their children do not apply their view of eternal justice when dealing with their children. Perhaps such parents are letting their children off too easy by giving them only twenty or thirty swats.[87]

This myth is reinforced by the myth that without endless punishment, there is no possibility of satisfying God's justice. It is amazing that traditionalists like Blanchard argue this way, because in doing so they really expose themselves. Obviously, the traditional assumption of infinite guilt is at work here, and that principle has already been refuted. Since finite sin does not require endless torment, there is no reason to think that God's justice will remain unsatisfied. The bigger problem exists for the traditionalist. In his scheme, God's justice is never satisfied because the lost must continue to suffer forever.[88] In the Bible, the justice of God is fully satisfied when the wrath of God is propitiated. This is why Christ is called the propitiation for our sins (1 Jn. 2:2). In the traditional view, God remains forever angry at the lost. Since his anger is never turned away or propitiated, clearly his justice is never satisfied. In short, it is not conditionalism that has trouble with the perfect justice of God—it is the traditional view that fails on this point! It is truly remarkable that traditional

---

[87] I am not suggesting that any parent discipline abusively like this; in fact, I mean to be sarcastic simply to illustrate the foolishness of arguing that a limited punishment is no punishment at all. If that were the case, even punishing our children excessively would be no punishment at all.

[88] A problem related to this is the problem of "eternal disharmony." The traditional view excludes any possibility of returning to the perfection and harmony of the original creation. In other words, once evil comes into the creation, God can never get it off his hands. See Dean 11.

theologians have failed to see that their own view of hell makes it impossible for God to satisfy the demands of his own justice.[89]

Another myth that perpetuates fear of conditionalism among traditionalists is the idea that without endless torment, the missionary zeal of the Church will falter.[90] As it turns out, this myth is only persuasive to traditionalists, because conditionalists have been doing evangelistic and missionary work right along with the best of the traditionalists. Denominations like the Advent Christian Church and the Seventh Day Adventists are among the most aggressively evangelistic. The Seventh Day Adventist Church is highly successful in evangelism and contributes generously to missionary work.[91] Regardless of one's opinion of these denominations from a doctrinal point of view, it is impossible to support the contention that conditionalism leads to a lack of missionary zeal or success.

The reason this myth is so credible to traditionalists is probably because their missionary motivation stems from their commitment to endless torment. They evangelize

---

[89] Traditionalists will say that eternal torment is *itself* the satisfaction of divine justice. But this cannot be true because God remains angry. Once God's justice is satisfied, so is his anger. Propitiation means the satisfaction of divine justice! In the final analysis, the endless wrath of God is *itself* the undoing of the traditional view of hell from a moral point of view. For over a century conservatives have rightly criticized liberals for denying that propitiation means the appeasement of divine wrath. How ironic that their own biblical defense of divine wrath destroys their belief in endless torment!

[90] John Piper, *Let the Nations Be Glad: The Supremacy of God in Missions* (Grand Rapids: Baker Book House, 1993) 120ff.

[91] Frank S. Mead, *Handbook of Denominations in the United States*, 10th ed. (Nashville: Abingdon Press, 1995) 37-40.

because they believe that their hearers will spend an eternity in hell if they do not seek to rescue them through the preaching of the gospel. There is real compassion reflected in this motivation, but it is not the only reason, or even the main reason, why Christians evangelize. It is also possible to evangelize from a positive motivation. In other words, some evangelize because they want to see others share in God's love, forgiveness, and blessing. Many people are attracted to the Christian faith because of these things primarily. Fear of judgment to come is certainly a biblical motivation to turn to God, but it is not the only motivation. Evangelism should be motivated primarily by love for others and secondarily by fear for their plight. Because traditionalists put so much emphasis on escaping endless torment, they logically think that removing that incentive will necessarily cripple missionary work. The truth is that it does not. Even without endless torment, there is still a fearful judgment to come and every reason to turn to God.

For traditionalists, endless torment is evangelism's silver bullet. They think that without it the cause of Christianity in the world will fail. Jonathan Edwards' sermon, *Sinners in the Hands of an Angry God*, is considered the masterpiece of evangelistic literature.[92] This sermon is the most famous in American history, and it is well-known for its stress on the endless torments of the damned.[93] What traditionalists

[92] Jonathan Edwards, *Sinners in the Hands of an Angry God* (Phillipsburg: P & R Publishing, 1992).

[93] The rhetorical power of Edwards' sermon is admired by traditionalists because of passages like the following: "It would be dreadful to suffer this fierceness and wrath of Almighty God one moment; but you must suffer it to all

CONCLUSION • Is Conditional Immortality A Heresy?

fail to consider is that sermons like this one probably turn as many people away from the Christian faith as they win to it. As stressed before, liberalism and cultism are often reactions to the extremities of the traditional view. The biblical view of judgment is more moderate and acceptable. The extremity of the traditional view often leads people to dismiss Christianity out of hand, because it runs so obviously counter to the notions of justice we use in everyday life. The problem is not simply that sinful people will not bow to God's standard of justice; many simply find the traditional concept of justice unintelligible.[94] After all, if God uses one standard of justice in human affairs based on finite guilt and another standard in eternal affairs based on infinite guilt, the average person is likely to feel uncertain about the Bible's ability to speak consistently about the matter of judgment.[95]

---

eternity. There will be no end to this exquisite horrible misery. When you look forward, you shall see a long forever, a boundless duration before you, which will swallow up your thoughts and amaze your soul; and you will absolutely despair of ever having any deliverance, any end, any mitigation, any rest at all. You will know certainly that you must wear out long ages, millions of millions of ages, in wrestling and conflicting with this almighty merciless vengeance; and then when you have so done, when so many ages have actually been spent by you in this manner, you will know that all is but a point of what remains. So that your punishment will indeed be infinite." (28-29)

[94] Those who oppose any concept of final judgment will not like conditional immortality any better than the traditional view. The central moral issue of the Christian faith is that every person will stand in the presence of God to be judged. There are many who would not struggle with the idea of accountability for their actions who would definitely struggle with the idea of an endless punishing for sin.

[95] Defenders of endless torment point out that human beings have no basis within themselves to criticize God's standard of justice. If God's justice demands endless torment, on what basis can that standard be criticized, since

A Call for Creaturely Humility

In any theological controversy, there must always be a concern for the practical implications of adopting one point of view over another. Aside from the obvious implications mentioned before, there is a practical reason to accept conditional immortality over the traditional view: The conditionalist view produces humility and mercy because of its more biblical view of human nature and the justice of God.

The doctrine of the immortality of the soul simply exalts mankind too much. If human beings are created immortal, then they are God-like by nature. There is no question that Christianity has the most exalted view of human nature among all the world's religions, but there is

---

without God the very concept of justice is unintelligible? I agree with this point, which is why my arguments are based primarily on what God has said about his justice, not on whether or not anyone likes those standards. Our emotions, however, are not without significance. Often an emotional response is a reflection of a serious problem at the heart of our beliefs. Emotions are the red flags of the conscience. If the conscience is properly trained by the truth of the Bible, our emotions will often give reliable signals. The almost universal emotional struggle with the idea of endless torment is, I believe, a valid indication that there is something very wrong with the traditional view. As long as our emotions are following the Bible and not leading it, the emotional arguments of conditionalists have significance and force. Traditionalists fail to do justice to the role of sanctified emotions in defending the truth of conditional immortality. They resort to branding any argument with an emotional coloring as sentimental. Many of these emotional arguments are really powerful extensions of sound biblical arguments. For example, will God and the redeemed really spend all eternity gleefully watching the damned writhe in hell like a cat in a microwave, as most traditionalists suggest? This rhetorical question certainly implies an emotional argument against endless torment. It does so, however, on the basis of the biblical idea that God is not a "cosmic torturer and terrorist."

CONCLUSION ▪ Is Conditional Immortality A Heresy?

also a danger inherent in this marvelous view of mankind. When the doctrine of the image of God in mankind is combined with the doctrine of the immortality of the soul, humans can become too special in their own eyes. The true glory of the Christian view of mankind is that we are mortal and perishing creatures by our creation but become immortal through the redemption of Christ. Humanity, by itself, is as weak and fragile as animal life. Conditionalism, of course, emphasizes our natural mortality and our dependence on God for eternal life. According to the Bible, "man, despite his riches, does not endure; he is like the beasts that perish." (Ps. 49:12)

Human pride will often take hold of anything that furthers an over-inflated view of self, including the notion of natural immortality. Non-Christians are offended by the idea that God considers them sinners, even though most suffer with guilt for the evils they have committed. When it comes to eternal life, most think they deserve it, even though they have never thanked God for the gift of earthly life. The truth is that God owes life to no one. Earthly life is a gift and eternal life is a gift. By contemplating our natural mortality and weakness, these things become self-evident.[96] The historical preoccupation with immortal

---

[96] The issue of natural mortality is vitally important to Calvinistic Christianity. The combination of predestination with eternal torment is simply an emotional load that very few have been able to bear in history. Calvinism has actually been its own worst enemy. By stressing both election and endless torment, the Calvinian tradition has really shot itself in the foot. Calvinism looks completely different from within the framework of conditional immortality. Since God did not owe us a first life, how can he be blamed for not choosing to grant everyone eternal life? Since immortality is not a part of our nature, we can hardly blame God for choosing those with whom he wants

soulism, however, has often clouded our vision of these things, making it possible to think more highly of ourselves than we ought to think (Rom. 12:3).[97]

The natural pride of the human heart is not something that is eradicated when people become Christians either. Often Christian theology is made to serve the natural pride of people, and instead of becoming humble, converts may even become more proud.[98] They can become intoxicated with a sense of self-importance that manifests itself in behavior that is unbecoming to the Christian profession. These observations are not meant to indict all traditionalists, for there are many good examples of humility among their numbers. But it is certainly true that a major doctrinal error like the immortality of the soul will have negative effects because it determines the Christian's view of himself.

---

to share his own immortality. Because of sin, those who are not chosen to life do not desire it anyway, so the reprobation of the non-elect is just God's way of giving them what they want—death (Prov. 8:36). Since the elect come to desire life by God's grace, God is really giving them something they would not have desired on their own. In the end, God is merciful even to those who are not chosen. They live for earthly life, so that is all they receive. They are justly punished for the sins of that one life and then mercifully terminated. This approach to Calvinism is certainly more reasonable and acceptable than the idea of predestination to endless torment. In summary, Calvinists will either rethink their doctrine of endless torment or they will have no future.

[97] The opposite error is to be found in religions like Buddhism and philosophies like existentialism. Because they do not accept the creation of mankind in God's image, they tend to make humanity less than it is. Pride is still in evidence, however, because each person becomes a god, answering to no one but himself and manufacturing his own meaning in life. In a strangely perverse way, these world views degrade humanity in order to justify the individual's exercise of divine prerogatives. In short, mankind achieves godhood through the evolutionary slime!

[98] This observation is based on many years of ministerial experience.

CONCLUSION • Is Conditional Immortality A Heresy?

The doctrine of endless torment also has a negative effect on the Christian mind because it determines the Christian's view of justice and mercy. The concept of mercy is difficult to learn when we are seeking to imitate a God who torments his enemies without mercy forever. People will become like the God they serve, so it should be no surprise that many traditionalists speak very glibly—even jokingly—about the torments of the lost in hell. The biggest problem, however, stems from the confusion within traditional circles that results from working with two different concepts of justice. When it comes to the temporal perspective, they believe that sins deserve a limited punishment. But when it comes to the eternal perspective, all sins deserve infinite punishing. This creates a tension that makes moral judgments very difficult. Depending on personality types, some will oscillate toward being fair because a punishment should fit the crime, and others will oscillate toward being judgmental because no punishment ever fits the crime, each crime being infinitely heinous.[99] Other less consistent personalities will simply ignore the confusion of trying to work with two opposing principles and will fall back on parental example or common sense in making moral judgments.

---

[99] This observation is also based on considerable pastoral experience. It is no secret that within churches that heavily stress endless torment there is a sizeable proportion of very judgmental people. Even relatively minor infractions are excessively censured, and legalism is often rampant. Such churches are especially attractive to perfectionistic personalities who are interested in building themselves up by judging others. Unfortunately, such churches fail to recognize that many of their interpersonal conflicts stem from a false view of divine justice that brings the worst out of people.

Christian communities that embrace conditional immortality become morally transformed by a new vision of the mercy and justice of God. They work with only one principle of justice, and they have many examples of God's mercy to teach them how to be merciful to others. Concern for fairness, proportion, and mercy in judging moral issues becomes the main objective. Those who were once judgmental relax and take more time evaluating moral issues and how to justly respond to those who have wronged them. Legalism also becomes less of a problem, since all sins are no longer viewed on the same moral level as equally deserving of infinite punishing. Best of all, they begin to look at those outside the community with God's eye of mercy. They become more effective in telling others about the Christian faith, less pushy, and more compassionate toward the sufferings of others. In short, they become more just and merciful.[100]

Conditional immortality is more than a just doctrinal formula about the final judgment of the world. It embodies the meaning of God's justice and mercy, our practice of justice and mercy, and the view of these things that will be conveyed to the world. Conditional immortality is certainly not a heresy. The doctrine of endless torment has spawned more heresies and negative reactions to the Christian faith than any other dogma of historic Christianity. Because of

---

[100] I have literally watched this kind of transformation take place in the congregation I have served. For ten years I taught the traditional view of hell and witnessed all the failings described above in myself and in others. After rejecting the traditional view and teaching conditionalism for only two years, I witnessed a remarkable transformation in the church.

this, the traditional view is really more worthy of the label of heresy than is conditional immortality. The biblical truth about hell is reasonable and acceptable. It was never given to torment Christians with thoughts about the endless suffering of friends and relatives who have gone into eternity without Christ. It was given to motivate Christians to tell those relatives about Christ before they face the first death so that they might not face the second death. But whatever the outcome of the Christian message in the lives of people, the justice and mercy of God should allow us to be at rest, knowing that the Judge of all the earth will do right.

BIBLIOGRAPHY

Adams, Jay. *The Grand Demonstration*. Santa Barbara: EastGate Publishers, 1991.

Bingham, D. Jeffrey. Rev. of *The True Image*, by Phillip E. Hughes. *Journal of the Evangelical Theological Society* 34 (1991): 397-398.

Blanchard, John. *Whatever Happened to Hell?*. Wheaton: Crossway Books, 1995.

Boettner, Loraine. *Immortality*. Phillipsburg: The Presbyterian and Reformed Publishing Co., 1956.

Brown, Harold O.J. "Will the Lost Suffer Forever?" *Criswell Theological Review* 4 (1990): 261-278.

Brzezinski, Zbigniew. *Out of Control: Global Turmoil on the Eve of the Twenty-First Century*. New York: Collier books, 1993.

Burton, Dan. "What Does It Mean to Be Evangelical?" *Christianity Today* 16 June 1989: 60-63.

Burton, Ernest De Witt. *Syntax of the Moods and Tenses in New Testament Greek*. Grand Rapids: Kregal Publications, 1994.

Crockett, William, ed. *Four Views on Hell*. Grand Rapids: Zondervan Publishing House, 1992.

Dean, David. A. "Is Conditionalism an Evangelical Heresy?" *Resurrection* 92.3 (1989): 10-11.

Edwards, David L., and John R. Stott. *Evangelical Essentials: A Liberal-Evangelical Dialogue*. Downers Grove: InterVarsity press, 1988.

Edwards, Jonathan. *Sinners in the Hands of an Angry God*. Phillipsburg: P & R Publishing, 1992.

Fudge, Edward William. *The Fire That Consumes: The Biblical Case for Conditional Immortality*. Carlisle UK: Paternoster Press, 1994.

Gomes, Alan W. "Evangelicals and the Annihilation of Hell." *Christian Research Journal* Spring (1991): 15-19.

Harmon, Kendall S. "The Case Against Conditionalism: A Response to Edward William Fudge." *Universalism and the Doctrine of Hell*. Ed. Nigel M. Cameron. Grand Rapids: Baker Book House, 1992. 191-224.

Hoekema, Anthony A. *The Bible and The Future*. Grand Rapids: Wm. B. Eerdmans Publishing Co., 1979.

Hughes, Phillip Edgcumbe. *The True Image: The Origin and Destiny of Man in Christ*. Grand Rapids: Wm. B. Eerdmans Publishing Co., 1989.

Johnson, A. F. "Conditional Immortality." *Evangelical Dictionary of Theology*. Ed. Walter A. Elwell. Grand Rapids: Baker Book House, 1984. 261.

Kantzer, Kenneth S. "Troublesome Questions." *Christianity Today*. 20 Mar. 1987: 45.

Kerr, D. W. "Immortality." *Evangelical Dictionary of Theology*. Ed. Walter A. Elwell. Grand Rapids: Baker Book House, 1984. 551-552.

Long, V. Phillips. Rev. of *Evangelical Essentials: A Liberal-Evangelical Dialogue*, by David L. Edwards and John R. Stott. *Presbyterion: Covenant Seminary Review* 17 (1991): 69-70.

Marshall, I. Howard. *The Gospel of Luke*. Grand Rapids: Wm. B. Eerdmans, 1978.

McKnight, Scott. "Eternal Consequences or Eternal Consciousness?" *Through No Fault of Their Own*. Ed. William V. Crockett and James G. Sigountos. Grand Rapids: Baker Book House, 1991. 147-157.

Mead, Frank S. *Handbook of Denominations in the United States*. Rev. Ed. Nashville: Abingdon Press, 1995.

Morey, Robert A. *Death and the Afterlife*. Minneapolis: Bethany House Publishers, 1984.

Morris, Leon. "Eternal Punishment." *Evangelical Dictionary of Theology*. Ed. Walter A. Elwell. Grand Rapids: Baker Book House, 1984. 369-370.

Nichols, James A. *Christian Doctrines: A Presentation of Biblical Theology*. Nutley: The Craig Press, 1970.

Nicole, Roger. "Annhilationism." *Evangelical Dictionary of Theology*. Ed. Walter A. Elwell. Grand Rapids: Baker Book House, 1984. 50-51.

--- . "Universalism: Will Everyone Be Saved?" *Christianity Today*. 20 Mar. 1987: 32-39.

North, Gary. Letter to ICE Subscribers. Feb. 1996.

--- . Letter to the author. 4 Aug. 1995

Peterson, Robert A. *Hell On Trial: The Case for Eternal Punishment.*" Phillipsburg: P & R Publishing, 1995.

Pinnock, Clark H. "The Destruction of the Finally Impenitent." *Criswell Theological Review* 4 (1990): 243-259.

--- . "Fire, Then Nothing." *Christianity Today.* 20 Mar. 1987: 40-41.

Piper, John. Letter to the author. 6 Jan. 1996.

--- . *Let the Nations Be Glad!: The Supremacy of God in Missions.* Grand Rapids: Baker Book House, 1993.

Reymond, Robert L. "Dr. John Stott On Hell." *Presbyterion: Covenant Seminary Review* 16 (1990): 41-59.

Ryrie, Charles C. Rev. of *The Fire That Consumes*, by Edward William Fudge. *Journal of the Evangelical Theological Society* 26 (1983): 457-458.

Shedd, W.G.T. *The Doctrine of Endless Punishment.* Carlisle: Banner of Truth Trust, 1990.

Stott, John R. W. "A Response to Professor Robert L. Reymond." *Presbyterion: Covenant Seminary Review* 16 (1990): 127-128.

Walvoord, John F. Rev. of *The Fire That Consumes*, by Edward William Fudge. *Bibliotheca Sacra* Oct. - Dec. 1984:563-564.

Wells, David F. "Everlasting Punishment." *Christianity Today* 20 Mar. 1987: 41-42.

Wenham, John W. "The Case for Conditional Immortality." *Universalism and the Doctrine of Hell.* Ed. Nigel M. Cameron. Grand Rapids: Baker Book House, 1992. 161-191.

www.ingramcontent.com/pod-product-compliance
Lightning Source LLC
Chambersburg PA
CBHW071307040426
42444CB00009B/1905